Providence, Rhode Island

Renee Browning

Contents

Articles

Attractions   **131**

Transport   **146**

References

Overview of Rhode Island

Rhode Island

State of Rhode Island and Providence Plantations	
Flag	Seal
Nickname(s): The Ocean State *Little Rhody*	
Motto(s): Hope	

Official language(s)	**De jure**: None **De facto**: English
Demonym	Rhode Islander
Capital	Providence
Largest city	Providence

Area	Ranked 50th in the US
- Total	1,214 sq mi (3140 km^2)
- Width	37 miles (60 km)
- Length	48 miles (77 km)
- % water	32.4
- Latitude	41° 09' N to 42° 01' N
- Longitude	71° 07' W to 71° 53' W
Population	Ranked 43rd in the US
- Total	1,053,209 (2009 est.)
- Density	1,012.3/sq mi $(390.78/\text{km}^2)$ Ranked 2nd in the US
Elevation	
- Highest point	Jerimoth Hill 812 ft (247 m)
- Mean	200 ft (60 m)
- Lowest point	Atlantic Ocean 0 ft (0 m)
Admission to Union	May 29, 1790 (13th)
Governor	Donald Carcieri (R)
Lieutenant Governor	Elizabeth H. Roberts (D)
Legislature	General Assembly
- Upper house	Senate
- Lower house	House of Representatives
U.S. Senators	Jack Reed (D) Sheldon Whitehouse (D)
U.S. House delegation	1: Patrick J. Kennedy (D) 2: James Langevin (D) (list)
Time zone	Eastern: UTC-5/-4
Abbreviations	RI US-RI
Website	http://www.ri.gov

> **Footnotes:** * Total area in acres
> is approximately 776957 acres (3144 km^2)

The **State of Rhode Island and Providence Plantations**, more commonly referred to as **Rhode Island** (🔊 /ˌroʊd ˈaɪlɨnd/ Wikipedia:Media helpFile:en-us-Rhode Island.ogg or English pronunciation: /rəˈdaɪlɨnd/), is a state in the New England region of the United States. It is the smallest U.S. state by area. Rhode Island borders Connecticut to the west and Massachusetts to the north and east, and it shares a water boundary with New York's Long Island to the southwest.

Rhode Island was the first of the thirteen original colonies to declare independence from British rule and the last to ratify the United States Constitution.

Rhode Island's official nickname is "The Ocean State," a reference to the state's geography, since Rhode Island has several large bays and inlets that amount to about 30% of its total area. Its land area is 1,045 square miles (2706 km^2), but its total area is significantly larger (in the United States, all seawater and ocean floors that are more than three nautical miles from land belong to the Federal Government.)

Origin of the name

Despite the name, most of Rhode Island is on the mainland United States. The name *Rhode Island and Providence Plantations* derives from the merger of two colonies, Providence Plantations and Rhode Island. *Providence Plantations* was the name of the colony founded by Roger Williams in the area now known as the City of Providence. *Rhode Island,* the other colonial settlement, was founded in the area of present-day Newport, on Aquidneck Island, the largest of several islands in Narragansett Bay.

It is unclear how Aquidneck Island came to be known as Rhode Island. In 1524, the explorer Giovanni da Verrazzano noted the presence of an island near the mouth of Narragansett Bay, which he likened to the Greek island of Rhodes. Although it is unclear to which island Verrazzano was referring, the pilgrims who later colonized the area decided to apply the moniker "Rhode Island" to Aquidneck Island. The earliest known use of the name "Rode Island" was in 1637 by Roger Williams. The name was officially applied to the island in 1644 with these words: "Aquethneck shall be henceforth called the Ile of Rods or Rhod-Island." The name "Isle of Rodes" is found used in a legal document as late as 1646.

Another popular origin theory is based on the fact that Adriaen Block, during his 1627 expedition, passed by Aquidneck Island, described in a 1625 account of his travels as "an island of reddish appearance" (in 17th-century Dutch, "een rodlich Eylande"). Dutch maps from as early as 1659 call the island "Roode Eylant", or Red Island. Historians have theorized that the island was named by the Dutch (possibly by Adriaen Block himself) for either the red autumn foliage or red clay on portions of the shore.

Roger Williams, a theologian who was one of the first to advocate freedom of religion, separation of church and state, abolition of slavery, and equal treatment to Native Americans, was forced out of the Massachusetts Bay Colony. Seeking religious and political tolerance, he and others founded "Providence Plantations" as a free proprietary colony. "Providence" referred to the divine providence

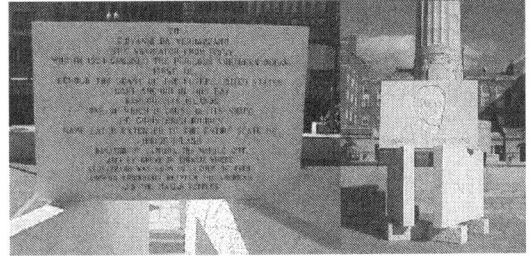

Verrazzano Monument, Providence, Rhode Island.

and "plantations" referred to a British term for a colony (people leave one place and are "planted" in another). Thus, this name bore no relation to the later Southern and Caribbean Islands slave plantations. Later on, Providence Plantations and Rhode Island were merged to form the Colony of Rhode Island and Providence Plantations.

"Rhode Island and Providence Plantations" is the longest official name of any state in the Union. On June 25, 2009, the General Assembly voted to allow the people to decide whether to keep the name or drop "Providence Plantations" due to the misperception that the name relates to slavery. A referendum election is to be held on this subject during the November 2, 2010 elections. Rhode Island's official state nickname is "The Ocean State," a reference to the state's geography (since Rhode Island has several large bays and inlets that amount to about 30% of its total area.)

Geography

Further information: List of counties in Rhode Island

Terrain Map of Rhode Island

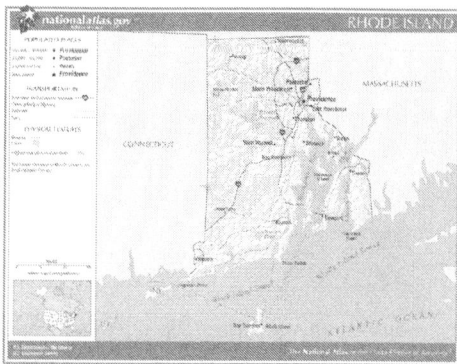

Map of Rhode Island, showing major cities and roads

Rhode Island covers an area of approximately 1,545 square miles (4,002 km²) and is bordered on the north and east by Massachusetts, on the west by Connecticut, and on the south by Rhode Island Sound and the Atlantic Ocean. It shares a narrow maritime border with New York State between Block Island and Long Island. The mean elevation of the state is 200 feet (60 m).

Nicknamed the Ocean State, Rhode Island has a number of oceanfront beaches. It is mostly flat with no real mountains, and the state's highest natural point is Jerimoth Hill, 812 feet (247 m) above sea level.

Located within the New England province of the Appalachian Region, Rhode Island has two distinct natural regions. Eastern Rhode Island contains the lowlands of the Narragansett Bay, while Western

Rhode Island forms part of the New England Upland. Rhode Island's forests are part of the Northeastern coastal forests ecoregion.

Narragansett Bay is a major feature of the state's topography. Block Island lies approximately 12 miles (19 km) off the southern coast of the mainland. Within the Bay, there are over 30 islands. The largest is Aquidneck Island, shared by the municipalities of Newport, Middletown, and Portsmouth. The second-largest island is Conanicut; the third-largest is Prudence.

Geology

A rare type of rock called Cumberlandite, found only in Rhode Island (specifically in the town of Cumberland), is the state rock. There were initially two known deposits of the mineral, but since it is an ore of iron, one of the deposits was extensively mined for its ferrous content.

Climate

Rhode Island is an example of a cold winter humid continental climate with hot, rainy summers and chilly winters. The highest temperature recorded in Rhode Island was 104 °F (40 °C), recorded on August 2, 1975 in Providence. The lowest recorded temperature in Rhode Island was -25 °F (-32 °C), on February 5, 1996 in Greene. Monthly average temperatures range from a high of 83 °F (28 °C) to a low of 20 °F (-7 °C).

Climate data for Rhode Island													
Month	Jan	Feb	Mar	Apr	May	Jun	Jul	Aug	Sep	Oct	Nov	Dec	Year
Record high °F (°C)	70 (21.1)	72 (22.2)	90 (32.2)	98 (36.7)	96 (35.6)	98 (36.7)	102 (38.9)	104 (40)	100 (37.8)	88 (31.1)	81 (27.2)	77 (25)	104 (40)
Average high °F (°C)	26 (-3.3)	39 (3.9)	48 (8.9)	58 (14.4)	69 (20.6)	77 (25)	83 (28.3)	81 (27.2)	73 (22.8)	63 (17.2)	52 (11.1)	42 (5.6)	59.3 (15.14)
Average low °F (°C)	20 (-6.7)	23 (-5)	30 (-1.1)	39 (3.9)	49 (9.4)	58 (14.4)	64 (17.8)	63 (17.2)	55 (12.8)	43 (6.1)	43 (6.1)	26 (-3.3)	42.8 (5.97)
Record low °F (°C)	-23 (-30.6)	-17 (-27.2)	1 (-17.2)	11 (-11.7)	29 (-1.7)	39 (3.9)	48 (8.9)	49 (9.4)	32 (0)	20 (-6.7)	6 (-14.4)	-12 (-24.4)	-23 (-30.6)
Precipitation inches (mm)	4.37 (111)	3.45 (87.6)	4.43 (112.5)	4.16 (105.7)	3.66 (93)	3.38 (85.9)	3.17 (80.5)	3.90 (99.1)	3.70 (94)	3.69 (93.7)	4.40 (111.8)	4.14 (105.2)	46.45 (1179.8)
Source:													

History

Main article: History of Rhode Island

Colonial era: 1636-1770

Main article: Colony of Rhode Island and Providence Plantations

In 1636, Roger Williams, after being banished from the Massachusetts Bay Colony for his religious views, settled at the tip of Narragansett Bay, on land granted to him by the Narragansett tribe. He called the site **Providence** and declared it a place of religious freedom. Detractors of the idea of liberty of conscience sometimes referred to it as "Rogue's Island". In 1638, after conferring with Williams, Anne Hutchinson, William Coddington, John Clarke,

Roger Williams and Narragansett Indians

Philip Sherman, and other religious dissidents settled on Aquidneck Island (then known as Rhode Island), which was purchased from the local natives, who called it Pocasset. The settlement of Portsmouth was governed by the Portsmouth Compact. The southern part of the island became the separate settlement of Newport after disagreements among the founders.

Samuel Gorton purchased the Native American lands at Shawomet in 1642, precipitating a military dispute with the Massachusetts Bay Colony. In 1644, Providence, Portsmouth, and Newport united for their common independence as the Colony of Rhode Island and Providence Plantations, governed by an elected council and "president". Gorton received a separate charter for his settlement in 1648, which he named Warwick after his patron. These allied colonies were united in the charter of 1663, used as the state constitution until 1842.[citation needed]

Although Rhode Island remained at peace with the Native Americans, the relationship between the other New England colonies and the Native Americans was more strained, and sometimes led to bloodshed, despite attempts by the Rhode Island leadership to broker peace. During King Philip's War (1675–1676), both sides regularly violated Rhode Island's neutrality. The war's largest battle occurred in Rhode Island, when a force of Massachusetts, Connecticut and Plymouth militia under General Josiah Winslow invaded and destroyed the fortified Narragansett Indian village in the Great Swamp in southern Rhode Island, on December 19, 1675. The Narragansett also invaded, and burnt down several of the cities of Rhode Island, including Providence, although they allowed the population to leave first. Also in one of the final actions of the war, troops from Connecticut hunted down and killed "King Philip", as they called the Wampanoag war-leader Metacom, on Rhode Island's territory.

The colony was amalgamated into the Dominion of New England in 1686, as James II of England attempted to enforce royal authority over the autonomous colonies in British North America. After the Glorious Revolution of 1688, the colony regained its independence under the Royal Charter. The bedrock of the economy continued to be agriculture, especially dairy farming, and fishing. Lumber and shipbuilding also became major industries. Slaves were introduced at this time, although there is no record of any law relegalising slave-holding. Ironically, the colony later prospered under the slave trade, by distilling rum to sell in Africa as part of a profitable triangular trade in slaves and sugar with the Caribbean.

Rhode Island was the first of the thirteen colonies to renounce its allegiance to the British Crown, on May 4, 1776. It was also the last colony of the thirteen colonies to ratify the United States Constitution on May 29, 1790 once assurances were made that a Bill of Rights would become part of the Constitution. As the home of Brown University, Rhode Island is one of only eight states hosting a colonial college chartered on its territory prior to the American Revolution.

Revolution to industrialization: 1770–1860

Rhode Island's tradition of independence and dissent gave it a prominent role in the American Revolution. In 1772, the first bloodshed of the American Revolution took place in Rhode Island when a band of Providence residents attacked a grounded British ship for enforcing unpopular British trade regulations. This incident would come to be known as the Gaspee Affair. Rhode Island was the first of the original thirteen colonies to declare its independence from Great Britain (May 4, 1776), and the last to ratify the Constitution, doing the latter only after being threatened with having its exports taxed as a foreign nation.

King Philip's Seat," a Native American meeting place on Mount Hope.

During the Revolution, the British occupied Newport. A combined Franco-American force fought to drive them off of Aquidneck Island. Portsmouth was the site of the first African American military unit, the 1st Rhode Island Regiment, to fight for the U.S. in the Battle of Rhode Island August 29, 1778. The arrival of a far superior French fleet forced the British to scuttle their own ships, rather than surrender them to the French.

The celebrated march of 1781 to Yorktown, Virginia that ended with the defeat of the British at the Siege of Yorktown and the Battle of the Chesapeake began in Newport, Rhode Island under the joint command of General George Washington who led American soldiers and the Comte de Rochambeau who led French soldiers sent by King Louis XVI.

These allied forces spent one year in Providence, Rhode Island, including at Brown University's University Hall, preparing for an opportune moment to begin their decisive march. Several patriots residing in Rhode Island were involved in the American Revolution, including Royal Governor Samuel Ward, Royal Governor and first Brown University Chancellor Stephen Hopkins, the Reverend James Manning, General James Mitchell Varnum, John Brown, Dr. Solomon Drowne, Yale College president Ezra Stiles and first United States Senator from Rhode Island Theodore Foster.

The Industrial Revolution began in America in 1787 when Thomas Somers reproduced textile machine plans he imported from England. He helped to produce the Beverly Cotton Manufactory, which Moses Brown of Providence took an interest in. Teaming up with Samuel Slater, Moses Brown helped to create the second cotton mill in America, a water-powered textile mill. As the Industrial Revolution moved large numbers of workers into the cities, a permanently landless, and

Providence in the mid-19th century.

therefore voteless, class developed. By 1829, 60% of the state's free white males were ineligible to vote.

Abandoned mill outside Newport (1968)

Several attempts had been made to address this problem, but none were successful. In 1842, Thomas Dorr drafted a liberal constitution which was passed by popular referendum. However, the conservative sitting governor, Samuel Ward King, opposed the people's wishes, leading to the Dorr Rebellion. Although this was not a success, a modified version of the constitution was passed in November, which allowed any white male to vote if he owned land or could pay a $1 poll tax.

In addition to industrialization, Rhode Island was heavily involved in the slave trade during the post-revolution era. Slavery was extant in the state as early as 1652, and by 1774, the slave population of Rhode Island was 6.3%, nearly twice as high as any other New England colony. In the late 18th century, several Rhode Island merchant families began actively engaging in the triangle slave trade. Notable among these was brothers John and Nicholas of the Brown family, for whom Brown University is named, although some Browns, particularly Moses, became prominent abolitionists. In the years after the Revolution, Rhode Island merchants controlled between 60% and 90% of the American trade in African slaves.

Civil War to Progressive Era: 1860–1929

During the Civil War, Rhode Island was the first Union state to send troops in response to President Lincoln's request for help from the states. Rhode Island furnished 25,236 fighting men, of whom 1,685 died. On the home front, Rhode Island, along with the other northern states, used its industrial capacity to supply the Union Army with the materials it needed to win the war. The United States Naval Academy moved here temporarily during the war.

In 1866, Rhode Island abolished racial segregation in the public schools throughout the state.

Post-war immigration increased the population. From the 1860s to the 1880s, most immigrants were from England, Ireland, Germany, Sweden, and Quebec. Toward the end of the century, however, most immigrants were from Eastern Europe and the Mediterranean. At the turn of the century, Rhode Island had a booming economy, which fed the demand for immigration. In the years leading up to World War I, Rhode Island's constitution remained reactionary, in contrast to the more progressive reforms that were occurring in the rest of the country. The state never ratified the 18th Amendment establishing national prohibition of alcohol.

During World War I, Rhode Island furnished 28,817 troops, of whom 612 died. After the war, the state was hit hard by the Spanish Influenza. In the 1920s and 1930s, rural Rhode Island saw a surge in Ku Klux Klan membership, largely in reaction to the large waves of immigrants moving to the state. The Klan is believed to be responsible for burning the Watchman Industrial School in Scituate, which was a school for African American children.

Growth in the modern era: 1929–present

In the 20th century, the state continued to grow, though the decline in industry devastated many urban areas. These areas were affected further, as with the rest of the country's urban areas, by construction of Interstate highways through city cores and the suburbanization caused by it and by the GI Bill.

Rhode Island's continued growth and modernization led to the creation of an urban mass transit system and improved health and sanitation programs.[citation needed]

Since the Great Depression, the Rhode Island Democratic Party has dominated local politics. Rhode Island has comprehensive health insurance for low-income children, and a large social safety net. Many urban areas still have a high rate of children in poverty. Due to an influx of residents from Boston, increasing housing costs have resulted in more homeless in Rhode Island.

The Republican Party, virtually non-existent in the state legislature, has successfully nominated state-wide "good government" reform candidates who criticize the state's high taxes and the excesses of the Democratic Party. Current Governor Donald Carcieri of East Greenwich, and former Mayor Vincent A. "Buddy" Cianci of Providence (who later became an independent political boss, and was convicted on RICO charges) ran as Republican reform candidates.

In recent yearsWikipedia:Manual_of_Style_(dates_and_numbers)#Chronological_items former Speaker of the House John Harwood, State Senator John Celona, and State Senate President William Irons were forced to resign amid scandals.[citation needed] In 2003, a nightclub fire in West Warwick claimed one hundred lives and caught national attention. The fire resulted in criminal sentences.

In March, 2010, areas of the state received record flooding due to rising rivers from heavy rain. The first period of rainy weather in mid-March caused localized flooding, but just two weeks later, more rain caused more widespread flooding in many towns, especially south of Providence. Rain totals on March 29–30, 2010 exceeded 14 inches in many locales, resulting in the inundation of area rivers - especially the Pawtuxet River which runs through central Rhode Island.

The overflow of the Pawtuxet River, nearly 11 feet (3.4 m) above flood stage, submerged a sewage plant and closed a five mile (8 km) stretch of Interstate 95. In addition, it flooded two shopping malls, numerous businesses, and many homes in Warwick, West Warwick, Cranston, and Westerly;Amtrak service between New York and Boston was also suspended during this period. Following the flood, Rhode Island was in a state of emergency for two days and President Obama came to neighboring Massachusetts to assess the damage; FEMA was also called in to help flood victims. As of June 2010, one of the malls has not reopened and many other places are still working to reopen.

Law and government

Presidential elections results

Year	Republican	Democratic
2008	35.21%	**63.13%**
	165,391	*296,571*
2004	38.67%	**59.42%**
	169,046	*259,760*
2000	31.91%	**60.99%**
	130,555	*249,508*
1996	26.82%	**59.71%**
	104,683	*233,050*
1992	29.02%	**47.04%**
	131,601	*213,299*
1988	43.93%	**55.64%**
	177,761	*225,123*

The capital of Rhode Island is Providence. The state's current governor is Donald L. Carcieri (R), and the lieutenant governor is Elizabeth H. Roberts. Its United States Senators are Jack Reed (D) and Sheldon Whitehouse (D). Rhode Island's two United States Congressmen are Patrick J. Kennedy (D-1) and Jim Langevin (D-2). *See congressional districts map.*

Rhode Island is one of a few states that does not have an official Governor's residence. *See List of Rhode Island Governors.*

The state legislature is the Rhode Island General Assembly, consisting of the 75-member House of Representatives and the 38-member Senate. Both houses of the bicameral body are currently dominated by the Democratic Party.

Because Rhode Island's population barely crosses the threshold for additional votes in both the federal House and electoral college, it is well represented relative to its population, with the eighth-highest number of electoral votes and second-highest number of House Representatives per resident. Based on its area, Rhode Island even has the highest density of electoral votes.

Federally, Rhode Island is one of the most reliably Democratic states during presidential elections, regularly giving the Democratic nominees one of their best showings. In the 1980 U.S. Presidential Election, Rhode Island was one of only 6 states to vote against Ronald Reagan. Reagan did carry Rhode Island in his 49-state victory in 1984, but the state was the second weakest of the states Reagan won. Rhode Island was the Democrats' leading state in 1988 and 2000, and second-best in 1996 and 2004. The state was devoted to Republicans until 1908, but has only strayed from the Democrats 7 times in the 24 elections that have followed. In 2004, Rhode Island gave John Kerry more than a 20-percentage-point margin of victory (the third-highest of any state), with 59.4% of its vote. All but three of Rhode Island's 39 cities and towns voted for the Democratic candidate. The only exceptions were East Greenwich, West Greenwich and Scituate. In 2008, Rhode Island gave Barack Obama a 29-percentage-point margin of victory (the third-highest of any state), with 64% of its vote. All of Rhode Island's 39 cities and towns voted for the Democratic candidate, except for Scituate.

Rhode Island has abolished capital punishment, making it one of 15 states that have done so. Rhode Island abolished the death penalty very early, just after Michigan (the first state to abolish it), and carried out its last execution in the 1840s. As of November 2009 Rhode Island is no longer one of two states in which prostitution is legal, provided it took place indoors. In a 2009 study Rhode Island was listed as the 9th safest state in the country.

Rhode Island has some of the highest taxes in the country, particularly its property taxes, ranking seventh in local and state taxes, and sixth in real estate taxes.

Rhode Island is the third state in the United States to pass legislation to allow the use of medical marijuana.

Further information: Political party strength in Rhode Island

Demographics

Historical populations		
Census	Pop.	%±
1790	68825	—
1800	69122	0.4%
1810	76931	11.3%
1820	83059	8.0%
1830	97199	17.0%
1840	108830	12.0%
1850	147545	35.6%
1860	174620	18.4%
1870	217353	24.5%
1880	276531	27.2%
1890	345506	24.9%
1900	428556	24.0%
1910	542610	26.6%
1920	604397	11.4%
1930	687497	13.7%
1940	713346	3.8%
1950	791896	11.0%
1960	859488	8.5%
1970	946725	10.1%
1980	947154	0%
1990	1003464	5.9%
2000	1048319	4.5%
Est. 2009	1053209	0.5%

	Demographics of Rhode Island (csv) [1]				
By race	**White**	**Black**	**AIAN***	**Asian**	**NHPI***
2000 (total population)	90.96%	6.45%	1.07%	2.74%	0.19%
2000 (Hispanic only)	7.14%	1.42%	0.18%	0.08%	0.07%
2005 (total population)	90.16%	7.07%	1.09%	3.07%	0.21%
2005 (Hispanic only)	9.12%	1.49%	0.22%	0.08%	0.08%
Growth 2000–05 (total population)	1.76%	12.52%	4.91%	15.09%	9.93%
Growth 2000–05 (non-Hispanic only)	-0.75%	13.80%	1.03%	15.44%	8.90%
Growth 2000–05 (Hispanic only)	31.21%	7.98%	24.03%	3.78%	11.64%
* AIAN is American Indian or Alaskan Native; NHPI is Native Hawaiian or Pacific Islander					

The center of population of Rhode Island is located in Providence County, in the city of Cranston. A corridor of population can be seen from the Providence area, stretching northwest following the Blackstone River to Woonsocket, where nineteenth-century mills drive industry and development. According to the U.S. Census Bureau, as of 2005, Rhode Island had an estimated population of 1,076,189, which is a decrease of 3,727, or 0.3%, from the prior year and an increase of 27,870, or 2.7%, since the year 2000. This includes a natural increase since the last census of 15,220 people (that is 66,973 births minus 51,753 deaths) and an increase due to net migration of 14,001 people into the state. Immigration from outside the United States resulted in a net increase of 18,965 people, and migration within the country produced a net decrease of 4,964 people.

The five largest ancestry groups in Rhode Island are:

- 19% Italian
- 19% Irish
- 17.3% French Canadian
- 12% English
- 8.7% Portuguese

Hispanics in the state make up 11% of the population, predominantly Puerto Rican, Dominican and with several Central American populations.

According to the 2000 U.S. Census, 8.07% of the population aged 5 and older speaks Spanish at home, while 3.80% speaks Portuguese, 1.96% French, and 1.39% Italian.

6.1% of Rhode Island's population were reported as under 5, 23.6% under 18, and 14.5% were 65 or older. Females made up approximately 52% of the population.

Rhode Island has a higher percentage of Americans of Portuguese ancestry (who dominate Bristol County), including Portuguese Americans and Cape Verdean Americans than any other state in the nation. Additionally, the state also has the highest percentage of Liberian immigrants, with more than 15,000 residing. French Canadians form a large part of northern Providence County whereas Irish Americans have a strong presence in Newport and Kent counties. Yankees of English ancestry still have a presence in the state as well, especially in Washington county, and are often referred to as "Swamp Yankees". African immigrants, including Cape Verdean Americans, Liberian Americans, Nigerian Americans and Ghanaian Americans, form significant and growing communities in Rhode Island. Although Rhode Island has the smallest total area of all fifty states, it has the second highest population density in the Union, second only to New Jersey.

Religion

The religious affiliations of the people of Rhode Island are:

- Christian – 87.5%
  - Roman Catholic – 49% (Per 2008 ARIS document)
  - Protestant – 21.6%
    - Episcopalian – 8.1%
    - Baptist – 6.3%
    - Evangelical – 4%
    - other – 3.2%
  - Other Christian – 2.3%
- Self-identified non-religious – 6%
- Other religions – 4.5%

The largest single Protestant denominations are the Episcopalians with 26,756 and the Baptists with 20,997 adherents.

The Jewish community of Rhode Island is centered in the Providence area, however the Touro Synagogue in Newport is the oldest existing synagogue in the United States.

Grace Church, a historic church at 175 Mathewson Street in Providence, Rhode Island.

Rhode Island has the highest percentage of Roman Catholics in the nation mainly due to large Irish, Italian, and French Canadian immigration in the past (these three groups form roughly 55%–60% of the state population); recently, significant Portuguese (though Portuguese communities have existed since the mid 19th century) and various Hispanic communities (these two groups form roughly 20% of the state population) have also been established in the state. Though it has the highest overall Catholic percentage of any state, none of Rhode Island's individual counties ranks among the 10 most Catholic in the United States, as Catholics are very evenly spread throughout the state.

Rhode Island and Utah are the only two states in which a majority of the population are members of a single religious body.

Cities and towns

Main article: Cities and towns in Rhode Island

See also: Rhode Island locations by per capita income

See also: Category:Villages in Rhode Island

There are 39 cities and towns in Rhode Island. Major population centers today result from historical factors — with the advent of the water-powered mill development took place predominantly along the Blackstone, Seekonk, and Providence Rivers.

A historic side street in Newport

Ranked by population, the state's 15 largest municipalities are:

1. Providence (175,255)
2. Warwick (85,925)
3. Cranston (81,479)
4. Pawtucket (72,998)
5. East Providence (49,123)
6. Woonsocket (43,940)
7. Coventry (33,668)
8. North Providence (32,411)
9. Cumberland (31,840)
10. West Warwick (29,581)
11. Johnston (28,195)
12. South Kingstown (27,921)
13. North Kingstown (26,726)
14. Newport (26,475)
15. Bristol (22,469)

In common with many other New England states, some Rhode Island cities and towns are further partitioned into villages that reflect historic townships which were later combined for administrative purposes. Notable villages include Kingston, in the town of South Kingstown, which houses the University of Rhode Island, and Wickford, in North Kingstown, the site of an annual international art festival.

Economy

The Rhode Island economy had a colonial base in fishing and farming, each of which respectively became shipping and manufacturing upon independence.

The Blackstone River Valley was a major contributor to the American Industrial Revolution". It was in Pawtucket that Samuel Slater set up Slater Mill in 1793, using the waterpower of the Blackstone River to power his cotton mill. For a while, Rhode Island was one of the leaders in textiles. However, with the Great Depression, most textile factories relocated to southern US states. The textile industry still constitutes a part of the Rhode Island economy, but does not have the same power that it once had.

Other important industries in Rhode Island's past included toolmaking, costume jewelry and silverware. An interesting by-product of Rhode Island's industrial history is the amount of abandoned factories - many of them now being used for low-income housing, elderly housing, condominiums, museums, and offices. Today, much of the economy of Rhode Island is based in services, particularly healthcare and education, and still to some extent, manufacturing.

The headquarters of Citizens Financial Group, the 14th largest bank in the United States, is located in Providence. The Fortune 500 companies CVS Caremark and Textron are based in Woonsocket and Providence, respectively. FM Global, GTECH Corporation, Hasbro, American Power Conversion, Nortek, and Amica Mutual Insurance are all Fortune 1000 companies that are based in Rhode Island.

Rhode Island's 2000 total gross state product was $33 billion, placing it 45th in the nation. Its 2000 *per capita* personal income was $29,685, 16th in the nation. Rhode Island has the lowest level of energy consumption per capita of any state. As of May 2010, the state's unemployment rate is 12.5%.

Health services are Rhode Island's largest industry. Second is tourism, supporting 39,000 jobs, with tourism-related sales at $3.26 billion in the year 2000. The third-largest industry is manufacturing. Its industrial outputs are costume jewelry, fabricated metal products, electrical equipment, machinery, shipbuilding and boatbuilding. Rhode Island's agricultural outputs are nursery stock, vegetables, dairy products and eggs.

Rhode Island's taxes were appreciably higher than neighboring states, because Rhode Island's income tax was based on 25% of the payer's federal income tax payment. Governor Carcieri has claimed that the higher tax rate had an inhibitory effect on business growth in the state and called for reductions to increase the competitiveness of the state's business environment. In 2010, the Rhode Island General Assembly passed a new state income tax structure that was then signed into law on June 9th, 2010 by

Governor Carcieri. The income tax overhaul has now made Rhode Island competitive with other New England states by lowering its maximum tax rate to 5.99% and has reduced the number of tax brackets to three. The state's first income tax was first enacted in 1971.

Transportation

A RIPTA bus at Kennedy Plaza.

The Claiborne Pell Newport Bridge

The Rhode Island Public Transit Authority (RIPTA), which has its hub in downtown Providence manages local bus transit for the state, serving 38 out of 39 Rhode Island communities. RIPTA has 58 bus lines, 2 tourist trolley lines known as LINK, and a seasonal ferry to Newport. The southern terminus of the MBTA commuter rail Providence/Stoughton Line is also in downtown Providence and connects to Boston. Ferry services link Block Island, Prudence Island, and Hog Island to the Rhode Island mainland.

The major airports are T. F. Green Airport in Warwick and Logan International Airport in Boston. The commuter rail is in the process of being extended to T.F. Green airport, which will link the airport to Providence and Boston by rail.

Interstate 95 runs diagonally across the state connecting major population centers, while the auxiliary interstate 295 provides a bypass around Providence. Narragansett Bay has a number of bridge crossings connecting Aquidneck Island and Conanicut Island to the mainland, most notably the Claiborne Pell Newport Bridge and the Jamestown-Verrazano Bridge. I-95 is one of the nation's deadliest highways, especially during the summer months. "Between 2004 and 2008, there were 36 fatal accidents on the highway, at a rate of nearly one accident for every mile."

Media

Main article: Media in Rhode Island

Education

Primary and secondary schools

Further information: Rhode Island schools

Colleges and universities

Main article: List of colleges and universities in Rhode Island

Rhode Island has several colleges and universities:

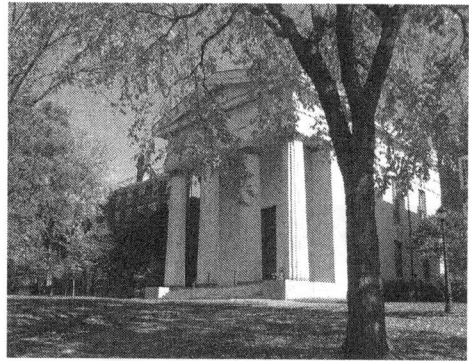

Manning Hall at Brown University

- Brown University
- Bryant University
- Community College of Rhode Island
- Johnson & Wales University
- Naval War College
- New England Institute of Technology
- Providence College
- Rhode Island College
- Rhode Island School of Design
- Roger Williams University
- Salve Regina University
- University of Rhode Island

Culture

Some Rhode Islanders speak with a non-rhotic accent that many compare to a "Brooklyn" or a cross between a New York and Boston accent ("water" becomes "wata"). Many Rhode Islanders distinguish the *aw* sound (English pronunciation: /ɔː/) as one might hear in New Jersey; e.g., the word *coffee* is pronounced [ˈkɔːfiː] *KAW-fee*.

Nicknamed "The Ocean State", the nautical nature of Rhode Island's geography pervades its culture. Newport Harbor, in particular, holds many pleasure boats. In the lobby of the state's main airport, T. F. Green, is a large lifesize sailboat, and the state's license plates depict an ocean wave or a sailboat.

Additionally, the large number of beaches in Washington County lures many Rhode Islanders south for summer vacation.

The state was notorious for organized crime activity from the 1950s into the 1990s when the Patriarca crime family held sway over most of New England from its Providence headquarters. Although the power of organized crime has greatly diminished in Rhode Island over the last 20 years, its residents are still stigmatized by popular perceptions of rampant graft and corruption that have haunted the state for decades[citation needed].

Rhode Islanders developed a unique style of architecture in the 17th century, called the stone-ender.

Rhode Island is the only state to still celebrate Victory over Japan Day. It is known locally as "VJ Day", or simply "Victory Day".

Food and beverages

Snail Salad from a local restaurant

Several foods and dishes are unique to Rhode Island and some are hard to find outside of the state.

Hot wieners, which are sometimes called *gaggers*, *weenies*, or *New York System wieners*, are smaller than a standard hot dog, served covered in a meat sauce, chopped onions, mustard, and celery salt.

Famous to Rhode Island is Snail Salad, which is served at numerous restaurants throughout the state. The dish is normally prepared "family style" with over five pounds of snails mixed in with other ingredients commonly found in seafood dishes.

Grinders are submarine sandwiches, with a popular version being the Italian grinder, which is made with cold cuts (usually ham, prosciutto, capicola, salami, and Provolone cheese).

Linguiça (a spicy Portuguese sausage) and peppers, eaten with hearty bread, is also popular among the state's large Portuguese community.

Pizza strips are prepared in Italian bakeries and sold in most supermarkets and convenience stores, they are rectangular strips of pizza without the cheese and are served cold. "Party pizza" is a box of these pizza strips.

Spinach pies are similar to a calzone but filled with seasoned spinach instead of meat, sauce and cheese. Variations can include black olives or pepperoni with the spinach, or broccoli instead of spinach.

As in colonial times, *johnny cakes* are made with corn meal and water, then pan-fried much like pancakes.

During fairs and carnivals, Rhode Islanders enjoy *dough boys*, which are plate-sized disks of deep fried dough sprinkled with powdered sugar (or pizza sauce).

Rhode Island zeppolas or zeppolis are different; traditionally eaten on Saint Joseph's Day (widely celebrated across the state), St. Joseph's Day zeppolis are doughnut-like pastries with exposed centers of vanilla pudding or ricotta cream, topped with a cherry.

As in many coastal states, seafood is readily available. Shellfish is extremely popular, with clams being used in multiple ways. The *quahog* (or *quahaug*, taken from the Narragansett Indian word "poquauhock" - see *A Key into the Language of America* by Roger Williams 1643) is a large clam usually used in a chowder. It is also ground and mixed with stuffing (and sometimes spicy minced sausage) and then baked in its shell to form a *stuffie*. Steamed clams are also a very popular dish.

Calamari (squid) is sliced into rings and fried and is served as an appetizer in most Italian restaurants, typically Sicilian-style, i.e. tossed with sliced banana peppers and with marinara sauce on the side.

Rhode Island, like the rest of New England, has a tradition of *clam chowder*. While both the white New England variety and the red Manhattan variety are popular, there is also a unique clear chowder, known as *Rhode Island Clam Chowder* available in many restaurants. According to Good Eats, the addition of tomatoes in place of milk was initially the work of Portuguese immigrants in Rhode Island, as tomato-based stews were already a traditional part of Portuguese cuisine, and milk was costlier than tomatoes. Scornful New Englanders called this modified version "Manhattan-style" clam chowder because, in their view, calling someone a New Yorker was an insult.

Perhaps the most unusual culinary tradition in Rhode Island is the *clam cake*. The clam cake (also known as a clam fritter outside of Rhode Island) is a deep fried ball of buttery dough with chopped bits of clam inside. They are sold by the half-dozen or dozen in most seafood restaurants around the state. The quintessential summer meal in Rhode Island is chowder and clam cakes.

Clams Casino originated in Rhode Island after being invented by Julius Keller, the maitre d' in the original Casino next to the seaside Towers in Narragansett. Clams Casino resemble the beloved stuffed quahog but are generally made with the smaller littleneck or cherrystone clam and are unique in their use of bacon as a topping.

According to a Providence Journal article, the state features both the highest number and highest density of coffee/doughnut shops per capita in the country, with 342 coffee/doughnut shops in the state. At one point, Dunkin' Donuts alone had over 225 locations.

The official state drink of Rhode Island is *coffee milk*, a beverage created by mixing milk with coffee syrup. This unique syrup was invented in the state and is sold in almost all Rhode Island supermarkets, as well as border states. Although coffee milk contains some caffeine, it is sold in school cafeterias throughout the state. Strawberry milk is also as popular as chocolate milk.

Frozen lemonade, a mixture of ice slush, fresh lemons, and sugar is popular in the summer, especially Del's Frozen Lemonade, a company based in Cranston.

Famous Rhode Islanders

Rhode Island State Symbols	
Animate insignia	
Bird(s)	Rhode Island Red Chicken
Fish	Striper Bass
Flower(s)	Violet
Tree	Red maple
Inanimate insignia	
Beverage	Coffee milk
Food	Rhode Island Greening Apple
Mineral	Bowenite
Rock	Cumberlandite
Shell	Northern Quahog
Slogan(s)	*Unwind*,"Hope"
Soil	Narragansett
Song(s)	*Rhode Island, Rhode Island, It's for Me*
Tartan	Rhode Island Tartan [2]Wikipedia:Link rot
Route marker(s)	

R.I.
3

State Quarter

Released in 2001

Lists of United States state insignia

Main article: Famous people from Rhode Island

Popular culture

Main article: Rhode Island in popular culture

The Farrelly brothers and Seth MacFarlane depict Rhode Island in popular culture, often making comedic parodies of the state. MacFarlane's television series Family Guy is based in a fictional Rhode Island city named Quahog, and notable local events and celebrities are regularly lampooned.

The movie *High Society*, starring Bing Crosby, Grace Kelly and Frank Sinatra, was set in Newport, Rhode Island.

The film adaptation of The Great Gatsby from 1974 was also filmed in Newport.

Jacqueline Bouvier Kennedy Onassis and John F. Kennedy were married at St. Mary's church in Newport, RI. Their reception was held at Hammersmith Farm, the Bouvier summer home in Newport.

Cartoonist Don Bousquet, a state icon, has made a career out of Rhode Island culture, drawing Rhode Island-themed gags in the *Providence Journal* and *Yankee* magazine. These cartoons have been reprinted in the *Quahog* series of paperbacks (*I Brake for Quahogs, Beware of the Quahog* and *The Quahog Walks Among Us*.) Bousquet has also collaborated with humorist and *Providence Journal* columnist Mark Patinkin on two books: *The Rhode Island Dictionary* and *The Rhode Island Handbook*.

Writer David Lafleche has written two books based in the semi-fictitious city of Thundermist: *Thundermist 04167* and *A Week Without Sunshine*. ("Thundermist" is accepted as a secondary name of Woonsocket.)

The 1998 film, Meet Joe Black was filmed at Aldrich Mansion in the Warwick Neck area of Warwick, RI.

Famous firsts in Rhode Island

Rhode Island is famous for being the first in many respects; some of the states most "famous firsts" include enacting the first law prohibiting slavery in North America on May 18, 1652. Slater Mill in Pawtucket was the first commercially successful cotton-spinning mill with a fully mechanized power system in America and was the birth place of the Industrial Revolution in the US. The oldest Fourth of July Parade in the country is still held annually in Bristol, Rhode Island. The first Baptist Church in America was founded in Providence in 1638. Ann Smith Franklin of the Newport Mercury was the first female newspaper editor in America (August 22, 1762). She was the editor of "The Newport Mercury" in Newport, Rhode Island. Touro Synagogue, the first synagogue in America, was founded in Newport in 1763. The first armed act of rebellion in America against the British Crown was the boarding and burning of the Revenue Schooner Gaspee in Narragansett Bay on June 10, 1772. The idea of a

Continental Congress was first proposed at a town meeting in Providence on May 17, 1774. Rhode Island elected the first delegates (Stephen Hopkins and Samuel Ward) to the Continental Congress on June 15, 1774. The Rhode Island General Assembly created the first standing army in the colonies (1,500 men) on April 22, 1775. On June 15, 1775, the first naval engagement of the American Revolution occurred between a Colonial Sloop commanded by Capt. Abraham Whipple and an armed tender of the British Frigate Rose. The tender was chased aground and captured. Later in June, the General Assembly created the first American Navy when it commissioned the Sloops *Katy* and *Washington*, armed with 24 guns and commanded by Abraham Whipple, who was promoted to Commodore. Rhode Island was the first Colony to declare independence from Britain on May 4, 1776. Pelham Street in Newport was the first in America to be illuminated by gaslight in 1806. The first strike in the United States in which women participated occurred in Pawtucket in 1824. Watch Hill has the nation's oldest carousel that has been in continuous operation since 1850. The motion picture machine (a machine showing animated pictures) was patented in Providence on April 23, 1867. The first lunch wagon in America was introduced in Providence in 1872. The first nine hole golf course in America was completed in Newport in 1890. The first state health laboratory was established in Providence on September 1, 1894 The Rhode Island State House was the first building with an all-marble dome to be built in the United States (1895–1901) The first automobile race on a track was held in Cranston on September 7, 1896. The first automobile parade was held in Newport on September 7, 1899 on the grounds of Belcourt Castle. The first NFL night game was held on November 6, 1929 at Providence's Kinsley Park. The Chicago (now Arizona) Cardinals defeated the Providence Steam Roller 16-0. And, in 1980, Rhode Island becomes the first and only state to decriminalize prostitution; prostitution is outlawed again in 2009. See (Prostitution in Rhode Island).

Sports

McCoy Stadium where the Pawtucket Red Sox play baseball

Rhode Island has two professional sports teams; both of which are top-level minor league affiliates for teams in Boston. The Pawtucket Red Sox, of the AAA International League, are an affiliate of the Boston Red Sox. The Pawtucket Red Sox play at McCoy Stadium in Pawtucket, Rhode Island and have won two league titles in 1973 and 1984. The other professional minor league team is the Providence Bruins, who are an American Hockey League affiliate of the Boston Bruins. The Providence Bruins play in the Dunkin Donuts Center

1884 Baseball Champion Providence Grays

University of Rhode Island's Meade Stadium and Ryan Center

in Providence and won the AHL's Calder Cup during the 1998–99 AHL season. The National Football League's New England Patriots play at Gillette Stadium in nearby Foxborough, Massachusetts, approximately 18 miles (29 km) north of Providence.

There are four NCAA Division I schools. The four teams all compete in four different conferences. The Brown University Bears compete in the Ivy League, the Bryant Bulldogs compete in the Northeast Conference, the Providence Friars compete in the Big East Conference and the Rhode Island Rams compete in the Atlantic-10 Conference. Three of the schools compete in the FCS division for college football. Brown, Bryant and Rhode Island are the three schools who currently field football teams.

Rhode Island also has a long and storied history for athletics. Prior to the great expansion of athletic teams all over the country Providence and Rhode Island in general played a great role in supporting teams. The Providence Grays won the first World Championship in baseball history in 1884. The team played their home games at the old Messer Street Field in Providence. The Grays played in the National League from 1878 to 1885. They defeated the New York Metropolitans of the American Association in a best of five game series at the Polo Grounds in New York. Providence won three straight games to become the first champions in major league baseball history. Babe Ruth played for the minor league Providence Grays of 1914 and hit his only official minor league home run for that team before being recalled by the Grays parent club, the Boston Red Stockings.

A now defunct professional football team, the Providence Steam Roller won the 1928 NFL title. They played in a 10,000 person stadium called the Cycledrome. A team by a similar name, the Providence Steamrollers, played in the Basketball Association of America; which would become the National Basketball Association.

From 1930 to 1983, America's Cup races were sailed off Newport, and the both extreme-sport X Games and Gravity Games were founded and hosted in the state's capital city.

The International Tennis Hall of Fame is in Newport at the Newport Casino, site of the first U.S. National Championships in 1881. The Hall of Fame and Museum were established in 1954 by James

Van Alen as "a shrine to the ideals of the game." The Hall of Fame Museum encompasses over 20000 square feet (1900 m^2) of tennis history, chronicling tennis excellence from the 12th century to today. The Hall of Fame has 13 grass courts, and is the site of the Hall of Fame Tennis Championships, the only professional tennis event played on grass courts in the United States. The first members of the Hall of Fame were inducted in 1955, and as of 2008, there are 207 players, contributors, and court tennis players in the Hall of Fame.

Landmarks

See also: List of Registered Historic Places in Rhode Island

The state capitol building is made of white Georgian marble. On top is the world's fourth largest self-supported marble dome. It houses the Rhode Island Charter of 1663 and other state treasures.

The First Baptist Church in America is the oldest Baptist church in the Americas, founded by Roger Williams in 1638.

Rhode Island State House

The first fully automated post office in the country is located in Providence. There are many mansions in the seaside city of Newport, including The Breakers, Marble House and Belcourt Castle. Also located there is the Touro Synagogue, dedicated on December 2, 1763, considered by locals to be the first synagogue within the United States (see below for information on New York City's claim), and still serving. The synagogue showcases the religious freedoms that were established by Roger Williams as well as impressive architecture in a mix of the classic colonial and Sephardic style. The Newport Casino

The Breakers Mansion

is a National Historic Landmark building complex that presently houses the International Tennis Hall of Fame and features an active grass-court tennis club.

Scenic Route 1A (known locally as Ocean Road) is in Narragansett. "The Towers", a large stone arch, is located in Narragansett. It was once the entrance to a famous Narragansett casino that burned down in 1900. The towers now serve as a tourist information center.

The Newport Tower has been hypothesized to be of Viking origin, although most experts believe it was a Colonial-era windmill.

See also

Main articles: Outline of Rhode Island and Index of Rhode Island-related articles

Bibliography

Primary sources

- Dwight, Timothy. *Travels Through New England and New York* (circa 1800) 4 vol. (1969) Online at: vol 1 [3]; vol 2 [4]; vol 3 [5]; vol 4 [6]
- McPhetres, S. A. *A political manual for the campaign of 1868, for use in the New England states, containing the population and latest election returns of every town* (1868) [7]
- Rhode Island's Geography and Climate [8]

Secondary sources

- Adams, James Truslow. *The Founding of New England* (1921) [9]
- Adams, James Truslow. *Revolutionary New England, 1691–1776* (1923)
- Adams, James Truslow. *New England in the Republic, 1776–1850* (1926)
- Andrews, Charles M. *The Fathers of New England: A Chronicle of the Puritan Commonwealths* (1919). Short survey by leading scholar.
- Axtell, James, ed. *The American People in Colonial New England* (1973), new social history
- Brewer, Daniel Chauncey. *Conquest of New England by the Immigrant (1926).*
- Coleman, Peter J. *The Transformation of Rhode Island, 1790–1860* (1963)
- Conforti, Joseph A. *Imagining New England: Explorations of Regional Identity from the Pilgrims to the Mid-Twentieth Century* (2001)
- Dennison, George M. *The Dorr War: Republicanism on Trial, 1831–1861* (1976)
- Hall, Donald, ed. Encyclopedia of New England (2005)
- Karlsen, Carol F. *The Devil in the Shape of a Woman: Witchcraft in Colonial New England* (1998)
- Lovejoy, David S. *Rhode Island Politics and the American Revolution, 1760–1776* (1969)
- McLaughlin, William. *Rhode Island: A Bicentennial History* (1976)
- Palfrey, John Gorham. *History of New England* (5 vol 1859–90) [10]
- Slavery in the North - Slavery in Rhode Island "Slavery in Rhode Island" [11]. Slavenorth.com. Retrieved July 31, 2010.
- Sletcher, Michael. *New England.* (2004).
- Stephenson, Nathaniel Wright. *Nelson W. Aldrich, a Leader in American Politics* (1930).
- WPA. *Guide to Rhode Island* (1939).
- Zimmerman, Joseph F. *The New England Town Meeting: Democracy in Action* [12]. (1999)

External links

- State of Rhode Island government website [13]
- Rhode Island State Databases [14] - Annotated list of searchable databases produced by Rhode Island state agencies and compiled by the Government Documents Roundtable of the American Library Association.
- Rhode Island [15] at the Open Directory Project
- Energy & Environmental Data for Rhode Island [16]
- USGS real-time, geographic, and other scientific resources of Rhode Island [17]
- U.S. Census Bureau [18]
- Rhode Island laws [19]
- Scituate Art Festival [20]
- Rhode Island State Facts [21]
- Detailed Historical Article from the 1911 Encyclopedia Britannica [22]
- Directory of filming locations in the state [23]
- Interactive Rhode Island Map Server [24]
- Old Postcards of Rhode Island [25]
- Old Interactive Rhode Island for children [26]

1. REDIRECT Template:Navboxes

Geographical coordinates: 41°42′N 71°30′W

frr:Rhode Island pnb:ﺁﺋﻠیﻨﺎﻥ زﻮﭬر

List of counties in Rhode Island

This is a list of the five **counties in the U.S. state of Rhode Island**. Rhode Island has the second lowest number of counties of any U.S. state (only Delaware has fewer, with three counties). Although Rhode Island is divided into counties, it does not have any local government at the county level. Instead, local government is provided by the eight cities and thirty-one towns.

Within Rhode Island, Washington County is often referred to as South County.

The colony of Rhode Island was established in the 17th century, and was the first of the thirteen original American colonies to declare independence from British rule in 1776, signaling the start of the American Revolution. The counties were all established before the Declaration of Independence.

The Federal Information Processing Standard (FIPS) code, which is used by the United States government to uniquely identify states and counties, is provided with each entry.

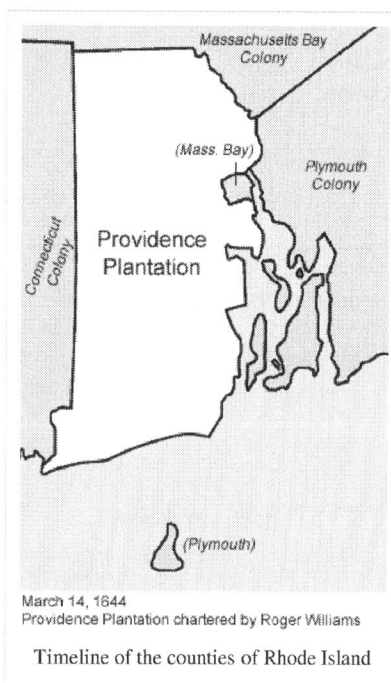

March 14, 1644
Providence Plantation chartered by Roger Williams

Timeline of the counties of Rhode Island

Rhode Island's code is 44, which when combined with any county code would be written as 44XXX. The FIPS code for each county links to census data for that county.

Alphabetical list

County	FIPS Code	County Seat (defunct)	Created	Origin	Etymology	Population (2000)	Area	Map
Bristol County	001 [1]	Bristol	1747	Created from land gained from Bristol County, Massachusetts after resolution of a boundary dispute between the two colonies.	City of Bristol, England	50648	45 sq mi (117 km^2)	

Kent County	003 [2]	East Greenwich	1750	Created from part of Providence County.	County of Kent, England	167090	188 sq mi (487 km^2)	
Newport County	005 [3]	Newport	1703	Formed as Rhode Island County in 1703. Renamed Newport County in 1729	Town (now city) of Newport, Wales	85433	314 sq mi (813 km^2)	
Providence County	007 [4]	Providence	1703	Formed in 1703 as Providence Plantations County. Renamed Providence County in 1729	Divine Providence	621602	436 sq mi (1129 km^2)	
Washington County	009 [5]	Wakefield	1729	Formed in 1729 as Kings County from part of Providence Plantations County. Renamed Washington County in 1781.	George Washington, American Revolutionary War general and first President of the USA	123546	563 sq mi (1458 km^2)	

References

Rhode Island County Map

History of Rhode Island

The **history of Rhode Island** includes the history of Rhode Island and Providence Plantations from pre-colonial times (1636) to modern day.

Pre-colonization

Native American inhabitants, including the Wampanoag, Narragansett, and Niantic tribes, occupied most of the area now known as Rhode Island. Most of the Native Americans were killed by European diseases and warfare with the Europeans. The Narragansett language died out for many years but was partially preserved in Roger Williams' the *A Key into the Languages of America* (1643). In the 21st century, the Narragansett tribe remains a federally recognized entity in Rhode Island.

King Philip's Seat," a Native American meeting place on Mount Hope, (Rhode Island)

In 1636, Roger Williams, after being banished from the Massachusetts Bay Colony for his religious views, settled at the tip of Narragansett Bay, on land granted to him by the Narragansett tribe. He called the site "Providence" and declared it a place of religious freedom. Detractors of the idea of liberty of conscience sometimes referred to it as "Rogue's Island".

In 1638, after conferring with Williams, Anne Hutchinson, William Coddington, John Clarke, Philip Sherman, and other religious dissidents settled on Aquidneck Island (then known as Rhode Island), which was purchased from the local natives, who called it Pocasset. The settlement of Portsmouth was governed by the Portsmouth Compact. The southern part of the island became the separate settlement of Newport after disagreements among the founders.

Another dissident, Samuel Gorton, purchased the Indian lands at Shawomet in 1642, precipitating a military dispute with the Massachusetts Bay Colony. In 1644, Providence, Portsmouth, and Newport united for their common independence as the Colony of Rhode Island and Providence Plantations, governed by an elected council and "president". Gorton received a separate charter for his settlement in 1648, which he named Warwick after his patron. These allied colonies were united in the charter of 1663.

In 1686, King James II ordered Rhode Island to submit to the Dominion of New England and its appointed governor Edmund Andros. This suspended the colony's charter but Rhode Island still managed to retain possession of it until Andros was deposed and the Dominion was dissolved. When William of Orange became King after the Glorious Revolution of 1688, Rhode Island's independent government resumed under the 1663 charter, which was used as the state constitution until 1842.

In 1693, the throne of William and Mary issued a patent extending Rhode Island's territory to three miles "east and northeast" of Narragansett Bay, conflicting with the claims of Plymouth Colony. This resulted in several later transfers of territory between Rhode Island from Massachusetts. (See History of Massachusetts.)

Colonial relations with Native Americans

The relationship between the New Englanders and the Native Americans was at first strained, but did not result in much bloodshed. The largest tribes that lived near Rhode Island were the Wampanoag, Pequots, Narragansett, and Nipmuck. One native named Squanto, from the Wampanoag tribe, stayed with the pilgrims and taught them many valuable skills needed to survive in the area. He also helped greatly with the eventual peace between the colonists and the natives.

Roger Williams meeting with the Narragansetts

Roger Williams had won the respect of his colonial neighbors for his skill in keeping the powerful Narragansetts on friendly terms with local white settlers. In 1637, the Narragansetts were even persuaded to form an alliance with the English in carrying out an attack that nearly extinguished the Pequots. However, this peace did not last long. By 1670, even the friendly tribes who had greeted Williams and the Pilgrims became estranged from the colonists, and smell of war began to cover the New England countryside.

The most important and traumatic event in 17th century Rhode Island was King Philip's War, which occurred during 1675–1676. King Philip (his British nickname, his real name was Metacomet) was the chief of the Wampanoag Indians. The settlers of Portsmouth had purchased their land from his father, Massasoit. King Philip first led attacks around Narragansett Bay, despite Rhode Island's continued neutrality, but later these spread throughout New England. A force of Massachusetts, Connecticut and Plymouth militia under General Josiah Winslow invaded and destroyed the fortified Narragansett Indian village in the Great Swamp in southern Rhode Island, on December 19, 1675. The Narragansett also invaded, and burnt down several of the cities of Rhode Island, including Providence, although they allowed the population to leave first. Also in one of the final actions of the war, troops from Connecticut led by Captain Benjamin Church hunted down and killed "King Philip", as they called the Narragansett war-leader Metacom, at Mount Hope, which is on Rhode Island's territory.

Revolutionary era 1775-1790

Rhode Island was the first British colony in America to formally declare its independence, doing so on May 4, 1776, a full two months before the national Declaration of Independence. Previously, in 1772 Rhode Islanders attacked the British warship the Gaspee as one of the first overt acts of rebellion in America. British naval forces under Captain James Wallace controlled Narragansett Bay for much of the Revolution, periodically raiding the islands and the mainland. The British raided Prudence Island for livestock and engaged in a skirmish with American forces, losing approximately a

Governor Joseph Wanton (being doused with punch and vomit) and other prominent Rhode Island merchants in "Sea Captains Carousing in Surinam," a 1755 painting

dozen soldiers. Newport remained a hotbed for Tory or Loyalist sympathizers who assisted the British forces. The state appointed General William West of Scituate to root out Tories in the winter of 1775-76. British forces eveuntally occupied Newport from 1777 to 1778 forcing the colonial forces to flee to Bristol.

The Battle of Rhode Island was fought during the summer of 1778 and was an unsuccessful attempt to expel the British from Narragansett Bay although few colonial casualties occurred. The Marquis de Lafayette called the action the "best fought" of War. The following year, the British, wanting to concentrate their forces in New York, abandoned Newport.

In 1780, the French under Rochambeau landed in Newport and for the rest of the war Newport was the base of the French forces in the United States. The French soldiers behaved themselves so well that in gratitude, the Rhode Island General Assembly repealed an old law banning Catholics from living in Rhode Island. The first Catholic mass in Rhode Island was said in Newport during this time.

Rhode Island was the last of the original 13 states to ratify the United States Constitution (May 29, 1790)—doing so after being threatened of having its exports taxed as a foreign nation. Rural resistance to the Constitution was strong in Rhode Island, and the anti-federalist Country Party controlled the General Assembly from 1786 to 1790. In 1788 anti-federalist politician and revolutionary general, William West, led an armed force of 1,000 men to Providence to oppose a 4 July celebration of the 9th state ratifying the Constitution. Civil war was narrowly averted by a compromise limiting the Fourth of July celebration.

Industrial Revolution and Dorr's reforms 1790-1860

In 1790 English immigrant, Samuel Slater founded the first textile mill in the United States in Pawtucket, Rhode Island (Slater Mill), and Slater became known as the father of the American industrial revolution. During the 19th century Rhode Island became one of the most industrialized states in the United States with large numbers of textile factories. The state also had significant machine tool, silverware, and costume jewelry industries.

As the Industrial Revolution moved large numbers of workers into the cities, a permanently landless, and therefore voteless class developed. By 1829, 60% of the state's free white males were ineligible to vote.

Samuel Slater (1768–1835) popularly called "The Father of the American Industrial Revolution"

Several attempts had been made to address this problem, but none passed. In 1842 Thomas Dorr drafted a liberal constitution which was passed by popular referendum. However the conservative sitting governor, Samuel Ward King, opposed the constitution, leading to the Dorr Rebellion. Although this collapsed, a modified version of the constitution was passed in November, which allowed any white male 21 or older to vote that owned land or could pay a $1 poll tax.

Slavery and abolition in Rhode Island 1652-1863

Prior to industrialization, Rhode Island was heavily involved in the slave trade during the post-Revolution era. Slavery was extant in RI as early as the 17th century. In 1652 Rhode Island passed the first abolition law in the thirteen colonies, banning African slavery. The law was not enforced by the end of the century. By 1774, the slave population of RI was 6.3%, nearly twice as high as any other New England colony. In the late 18th century, several Rhode Island merchant families (most notably the Browns, for whom Brown University is named) began actively engaging in the triangle slave trade. In the years after the Revolution, Rhode Island merchants controlled between 60 and 90 percent of the American trade in African slaves. The 18th century Rhode Island's economy depended largely upon the triangle trade, where Rhode Islanders distilled rum from molasses, sent the rum to Africa to trade for slaves, and then traded the slaves in the West Indies for more molasses.

While serving in the Rhode Island Assembly in 1774, Stephen Hopkins introduced a bill that prohibited the importation of slaves into the colony. This became one of the first anti-slavery laws in the new United States. In February 1784 the Rhode Island Legislature passed a compromise measure for gradual emancipation of slaves within Rhode Island. All children of slaves born after March 1 were to be "apprentices," the girls to become free at 18, the boys at 21. By 1840, the census reported only five

African Americans enslaved in Rhode Island. Using southern cotton Rhode Island manufactured numerous textiles used in the southern slavery throughout the early 19th century. By the mid-19th century, many Rhode Islanders were active in the abolitionist movement, particularly Quakers in Newport and Providence such as Moses Brown.

Civil War to Progressive era: 1860–1929

Main article: Rhode Island in the American Civil War

During the American Civil War, Rhode Island was one of the Union states. Rhode Island furnished 25,236 fighting men, of which 1,685 died. On the home front, Rhode Island, along with the other northern states, used its industrial capacity to supply the Union Army with the materials it needed to win the war. Rhode Island's continued growth and modernization led to the creation of an urban mass transit system, and improved health and sanitation programs. After the war, in 1866, Rhode Island abolished racial segregation throughout the state. Post-war immigration increased the population. From the 1860s to the 1880s, most of the immigrants were from England, Ireland, Germany, Sweden, and Quebec. Towards the end of the century however, most immigrants were from South and Eastern Europe, and the Mediterranean. At the turn of the century, Rhode Island had a booming economy, which fed the demand for immigration. In the years that lead up to World War I, Rhode Island's constitution remained reactionary, in contrast to the more progressive reforms that were occurring in the rest of the country. During World War I, Rhode Island furnished 28,817 troops, of whom 612 died. After the war, the state was hit hard by the Spanish Influenza.

In the 1920s and 30s, rural Rhode Island saw a surge in Ku Klux Klan membership largely among the native-born white population in reaction to the large waves of immigrants moving to the state. The Klan is believed to be responsible for burning the Watchman Industrial School in Scituate, Rhode Island, which was a school for African American children.

Great Depression to present: 1929–2010

Since the 1935 "Bloodless Revolution" in which Governor Theodore Francis Green and Democratic majorities in the state House and Senate replaced a Yankee Republican dominance that had existed since the middle of the 19th century, the Rhode Island Democratic Party has dominated state politics. Since then, the Speaker of the House, always a Democrat, has been one of the most powerful figures in government. The Democratic Party represented a coalition of labor unions, working class immigrants, intellectuals, college students, and the rising ethnic middle class. The Republican Party has been dominant in rural and suburban parts of the state, and has elected occasional "good government" reform candidates who criticize the state's high taxes and the excesses of Democratic domination. Cranston Mayors Edward D. DiPrete and

U.S. Senator and Governor,
T.F. Green

Stephen Laffey, Governor Donald Carcieri of East Greenwich, and former Mayor Vincent A. "Buddy" Cianci of Providence ran as Republican reform candidates.

The state income tax was first enacted in 1971 as a temporary measure. Prior to 1971 there was no income tax in the state, but the temporary income tax soon became permanent. The tax burden in Rhode Island, including sales, gasoline, property, cigarette, corporate, and capital gains taxes, remains among the five highest in the United States.

Rhode Islanders have overwhelmingly supported and re-elected Democrats to positions of authority, where issues involving education, health care, and liberal causes are promoted. As of 2010 Rhode Island has heavily Democratic controlled legislatures, and both U.S. Senators and Congressman, and all statewide offices other than governor are held by Democrats.

Population

Towns	1790	1810	1830	1860
Providence	6,380	10,071	16,836	50,666
Other 9 expanding towns	14,424	21,432	31,361	65,343
All Expanding Towns	20,804	31,503	48,197	116,009
Newport	6,716	7,907	8,010	10,508
16 Static Towns	37,133	35,709	39,064	50,992
6 Declining Towns	10,888	9,719	9,949	7,619
Rhode Island	68,825	76,931	97,210	174,620
Source: Coleman p 220				

I+ **The population of Rhode Island, 1790–1860**

See also

Main article: Historical outline of Rhode Island

- History of New England
- Colony of Rhode Island and Providence Plantations
- Thirteen Colonies

Regarding border disputes

- Washington County, Rhode Island
- Bristol County, Rhode Island
- History of Massachusetts
- History of Connecticut

External links

- Providence Journal [1]
- Rhode Island History [2]
- Rhode Island Naval History [3]
- 1853 History of Rhode Island (full text online) [4]
- State of Rhode Island and Providence Plantations at the end of the century [5] by Edward Field. History of the state, published in 1902. (Full text available online.)
- 1663 charter [6]

National Register of Historic Places listings in Rhode Island

This is a list of properties and districts listed on the **National Register of Historic Places in Rhode Island**. As of September 17, 2010, there are 738 listed sites in Rhode Island. All 5 of the counties in Rhode Island have listings on the National Register.

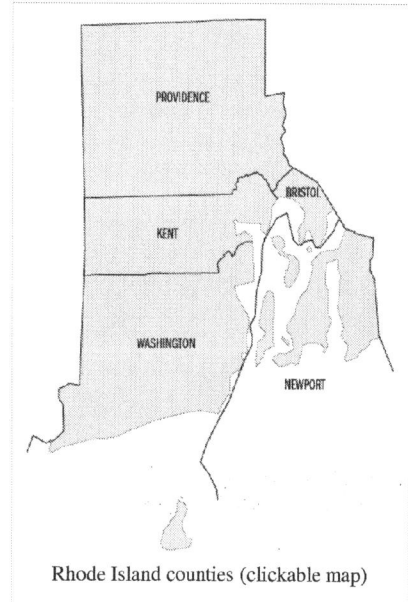

Rhode Island counties (clickable map)

Contents: Counties in Rhode Island

Bristol - Kent - Newport - Providence - Washington

Current listings by county

The following are approximate tallies of current listings by county. These counts are based on entries in the National Register Information Database as of April 24, 2008 and new weekly listings posted since then on the National Register of Historic Places web site. There are frequent additions to the listings and occasional delistings and the counts here are approximate and not official. New entries are added to the official Register on a weekly basis. Also, the counts in this table exclude boundary increase and decrease listings which modify the area covered by an existing property or district and which carry a separate National Register reference number. The numbers of NRHP listings in each county are documented by tables in each of the individual county list-articles.

Beavertail Light, Newport County

Joseph Reynolds House, Bristol County

	County	# of Sites
1	Bristol	24
2	Kent	77
3	Newport	118
4.1	Providence: Pawtucket	50
4.2	Providence: Providence (city)	158
4.3	Providence: Other	191
4.4	Providence: Duplicates	(1)
4.5	Providence: Total	398
5	Washington	125
	(duplicates)	(3)
	Total:	739

Arkwright Bridge, Providence County

Pawtucket City Hall, Pawtucket

See also

- List of National Historic Landmarks in Rhode Island

First Baptist Church in America

First Baptist Meetinghouse	
U.S. National Register of Historic Places	
U.S. National Historic Landmark	
Front elevation, 2008	
Location:	Providence, RI
Coordinates:	41°49′38″N 71°24′29″W
Built/Founded:	1775
Architect:	Joseph Brown; Multiple
Architectural style(s):	Georgian
Governing body:	Private
Added to NRHP:	October 15, 1966
Designated NHL:	October 9, 1960
NRHP Reference#:	66000017

The **First Baptist Church in America** is the **First Baptist Church of Providence, Rhode Island**, also known as **First Baptist Meetinghouse**. The oldest Baptist church congregation in the United States, it was founded by Roger Williams in Providence, Rhode Island in 1638. The present church building was erected in 1774-1775 and held its first meetings in 1776.

History

Roger Williams had been holding religious services in his home for nearly a year before he converted his congregation into a Baptist church in 1638. This followed his founding of Providence in 1636. For the next sixty years, the congregation met outside in nice weather or in congregants' homes. Baptists in Rhode Island through most of the 17th century declined to erect meetinghouses because they felt that buildings reflected vanity. Eventually, however, they came to see the utility of some gathering place, and they erected severely plain-style meetinghouses like the Quakers.

Roger Williams was a Calvinist, but within a few years of its founding, the congregation became more Arminian, and was clearly a General Six-Principle Baptist church by 1652. It remained a General Baptist church until it switched back to a Calvinist variety under the leadership of James Manning in the 1770s. Following Williams as pastor of the church was Rev. Chad Brown, founder of the famous Brown family of Rhode Island. A number of the streets in Providence bear the names of pastors of First Baptist Church, including Williams, Brown, Gregory Dexter, Thomas Olney, William Wickenden, Manning, and Stephen Gano. In 1700 Reverend Pardon Tillinghast built the first church building, a 400-square-foot (37 m^2) structure, near the corner of Smith and North Main Streets. In 1711 he donated the building and land to the church in a deed describing the church as General Six-Principle Baptist in theology. In 1736 the congregation built its second meetinghouse on an adjoining lot at the corner of Smith and North Main Streets. This building was about 40 x 40 feet square.

When it was built in 1774-1775, the current Meeting House represented a dramatic departure from the traditional Baptist meetinghouse style. It was the first Baptist meetinghouse to have a steeple and bell, making it more like Anglican and Congregational church buildings. The builders were part of a movement among Baptists in the urban centers of Boston, Newport, New York, and Philadelphia to bring respectability and recognition to Baptists.

Association with Brown University

Central to that movement was the creation of an educated ministry and the founding of a college. The Philadelphia Baptist Association sent Dr. James Manning to Rhode Island to found the College in the English Colony of Rhode Island and Providence Plantations (later renamed Brown University) in 1764. Beginning in Warren, the college then relocated to Providence in 1770. The college president, the Reverend Manning was called to be the pastor of the Providence church in 1771, and during his ministry the Meeting House was erected "for the publick worship of Almighty God and also for holding commencement in." Brown presidents Maxcy and Wayland also served as ministers at the church. The Brown family that soon gave its name to the University were prominent members of the Church, descendants of founders of the Church, as well as the Rhode Island Colony. Although the university is now secular, in honor of its history and tradition, the Meeting House continues, as it has since 1776, to be the site for Brown University's undergraduate commencement.

Construction began on the building in the summer of 1774, and it was the biggest building project in New England at the time. Due to the closure of the Massachusetts ports by the British as punishment for the Boston Tea Party, out-of-work ship builders and carpenters came to Providence to work on the Meeting House. The main portion of the Meeting House was dedicated in mid-May 1775, and the steeple erected in just three days in the first week of June. Notable additions to the Meeting House have included a Waterford crystal chandelier given by Hope Brown Ives (1792), a large pipe organ given by her brother Nicholas Brown, Jr., the younger (1834), the creation of rooms for Sunday school, fellowship hall, and offices on the lower level (1819–1859), and an addition to the east end of the Meeting House to accommodate an indoor baptistery (1884). The building was designated a National Historic Landmark in 1966.

Today

In addition to weekly worship services, the Meeting House has hosted concerts, talks, and lectures by world-renowned artists, performers, academics, and elected officials. Brown University continues to hold Commencement services in The Meeting House to this day.

Dan Ivins began his ministry in February 2006 as interim and was then called as settled minister on December 24, 2006. In 2001, history professor J.Stanley Lemons wrote a history of the church, entitled *FIRST: The History of the First Baptist Church in America*

Affiliations

The First Baptist Church in America is affiliated with the American Baptist Churches of Rhode Island (ABCORI) and the American Baptist Churches/USA (ABCUSA). The church actively supports the Rhode Island State Council of Churches, the National Council of Churches, the World Baptist Alliance, and the Baptist Joint Committee on Religious Liberty. Many members have served in various denominational, academic, and divinity school positions, including the presidency of Brown University.

Images

Settled ministers (sometimes simultaneous pastorships)

- Roger Williams, 1638–39
- Chad Brown, 1639-before 1650
- Thomas Olney, 1639–1652
- William Wickenden, 1642–1670
- Gregory Dexter, 1654–1700
- Pardon Tillinghast, 1681–1718
- Ebenezer Jenckes 1719-1726
- James Brown 1726-1732
- Samuel Winsor, 1733–1758
- Thomas Burlingame 1733-1764
- Samuel Winsor, Jr, 1759–1771
- James Manning, 1771–1791

- John Stanford, 1788–1789
- Jonathan Maxcy, 1791–1792
- Stephen Gano MD, 1792–1828
- Robert Pattison, 1830–36
- William Hague, 1837–40
- Robert Pattison,1840–1842
- James Granger, 1842–1857
- Francis Wayland, 1857–1858
- Samuel Caldwell, 1858–1873
- Edward G. Taylor, 1875–1881
- Thomas Edwin Brown, 1882–1890
- Henry Melville King, 1891–1906
- Elijah Abraham Hanley, 1907–1911
- John F. Vichert, 1912–1916
- Albert B. Cohoe, 1916–1920
- Arthur W. Cleaves, 1922–1940
- Albert C. Thomas, 1941–1954
- Homer L. Trickett, 1955–1970
- Robert G. Withers, 1971–1975
- Richard D. Bausman, 1976–1982
- Orland L. Tibbetts, 1983–1986
- Dwight M. Lundgren, 1983–1996
- Kate Harvey Penfield, 1987–1995
- Clifford R. Hockensmith, 1997–1999
- James C. Miller, 2000–2005
- Dan Ivins, 2006-

See also

- Oldest churches in the United States

External links

- The First Baptist Church in America [1]
- Meeting House info [2]

The Breakers

The Breakers	
U.S. National Register of Historic Places	
U.S. National Historic Landmark	

Rear elevation of The Breakers, 2009

Location:	44 Ochre Point Avenue, Newport, Rhode Island
Coordinates:	41°28′11″N 71°17′55″W
Built/Founded:	1893
Architect:	Richard Morris Hunt
Architectural style(s):	Italian Renaissance
Governing body:	Private
Added to NRHP:	September 10, 1971
Designated NHL:	October 12, 1994
NRHP Reference#:	71000019

The Breakers is a Vanderbilt mansion located on Ochre Point Avenue, Newport, Rhode Island, United States on the Atlantic Ocean. It is a National Historic Landmark, a contributing property to the Bellevue Avenue Historic District, and is owned and operated by the Preservation Society of Newport

County.

The Breakers was built as the Newport summer home of Cornelius Vanderbilt II, a member of the wealthy United States Vanderbilt family. Designed by renowned architect Richard Morris Hunt and with interior decoration by Jules Allard and Sons and Ogden Codman, Jr., the 70-room mansion boasts approximately 65000 sq ft (6000 m^2). of living space. The home was constructed between 1893 and 1895 at a cost of more than $7 million (approximately $150 million in today's dollars adjusted for inflation). The Ochre Point Avenue entrance is marked by sculpted iron gates and 30-foot (9.1 m) high walkway gates are part of a 12-foot-high limestone and iron fence that borders the property on all but the ocean side. The 250' x 120' dimensions of the five-story mansion are aligned symmetrically around a central Great Hall.

Part of a 13-acre (53,000 m²) estate on the seagirt cliffs of Newport, it sits in a commanding position that faces east overlooking the Atlantic Ocean.

History

View of The Breakers from the entrance gate

As the previous mansion on the property owned by Pierre Lorillard IV burned down in 1892, Cornelius Vanderbilt II insisted that the building be made as fireproof as possible and as such, the structure of the building used steel trusses and no wooden parts. He even required that the furnace be located away from the house, under Ochre Point Avenue; in winter there is an area in front of the main gate over the furnace where snow and ice always melt.

The designers created an interior using marble imported from Italy and Africa plus rare woods and mosaics from countries around the world. It also included architectural elements (such as the library mantel) purchased from chateaux in France. The Gold Room was originally constructed in France, disassembled, shipped in airtight cases, and re-assembled in place in Newport.

The Breakers is the architectural and social archetype of the "Gilded Age", a period when members of the Vanderbilt family were among the most prominent industrialists of America. Indeed, "if the Gilded Age were to be summed up by a single house, that house would have to be The Breakers." In 1895, the year of its completion, The Breakers was the largest, most opulent house in a summer resort considered the social capital of America.

Vanderbilt died from a cerebral hemorrhage caused from a second stroke in 1899 at the age of 55, leaving the Breakers to his wife, Alice Gwynne Vanderbilt. She outlived her husband by 35 years and died at the age of 89 in 1934. In her will, The Breakers was given to her youngest daughter Gladys essentially because Gladys lacked American property. Also, none of Alice's other children were interested in the property while Gladys had always loved the estate.

The Breakers survived the great New England Hurricane of 1938 with minimal damage and minor flooding of the grounds.

In 1948 Countess Gladys Széchenyi (1886–1965), the youngest daughter of Cornelius Vanderbilt II, leased the high-maintenance property to the non-profit Preservation Society of Newport County for $1 a year. The Society bought the Breakers outright in 1972 for $365,000 from Countess Sylvia Szapary, the daughter of Gladys. However, the agreement with the Society allows the family to continue to live on the third floor, which is not open to the public. Countess Sylvia lived there part time until her death on March 1, 1998. Gladys and Paul Szapary, Sylvia's children, summer there to this day, hidden from the hundreds of thousands of tourists who explore below.

Although the mansion is owned by the Society, the original furnishings displayed throughout the house are still owned by the family.

It is now the most-visited attraction in Rhode Island with approximately 300,000 visitors annually and is open year-round for tours.

In April 2009 the museum stopped offering personalized tours by tour guides due to a decision by management. Patrons now receive standard audio headsets.

Gardens

The pea-gravel driveway is lined with maturing pin oaks and red maples. The formally landscaped terrace is surrounded by Japanese yew, Chinese juniper, and dwarf hemlock. The trees of The Breakers' grounds act as screens that increase the sense of distance between The Breakers and its Newport neighbors. Among the more unusual imported trees are two examples of the Blue Atlas Cedar, a native of North Africa. Clipped hedges of Japanese yew and Pfitzer juniper line the tree shaded foot paths that meander about the grounds. Informal plantings of arbor vitae, taxus, Chinese juniper, and dwarf hemlock provide attractive foregrounds for the walls that enclose the formally landscaped terrace. The grounds also contain several varieties of other rare trees, particularly

Gardens at The Breakers

copper and weeping beeches. These were hand-selected by James Bowditch, a forester based in the Boston area. Bowditch's original pattern for the south parterre garden was determined from old photographs and laid out in pink and white alyssum and blue ageratum. The wide borders paralleling

the wrought iron fence are planted with rhododendron, laurel, dogwoods, and many other flowering shrubs that effectively screen the grounds from street traffic and give the visitor a feeling of complete seclusion.

Layout

Basement

- Laundry
- Staff's Restrooms

First Floor

- Entrance Foyer
- Gentlemen's Reception Room
- Ladies' Reception Room
- Great Hall (50 ft x 50 ft (15 m) x 50 ft) – Over each of the six doors which lead from the Great Hall are limestone figure groups celebrating humanity's progress in art, science, and industry: Galileo, representing science; Dante, representing literature; Apollo, representing the arts; Mercury, representing speed and commerce; Richard Morris Hunt, representing architecture; and Karl Bitter, representing sculpture

The Great Hall

- Main Staircase (though visitors may not use them)
- Arcade
- Library
- Music Room
- Morning Room
- Porch
- Lower Loggia
- Billiard Room
- Dining Room
- Marriage Chest
- Breakfast Room
- Pantry
- Kitchen

The library

Second Floor

- Mr. Vanderbilt's Bedroom
- Mrs. Vanderbilt's Bedroom
- Miss Gertrude Vanderbilt's Bedroom
- Upper Loggia
- Guest Bedroom
- Countess Szechenyi's Bedroom
- There are also two other small bedrooms located on the second floor.

The kitchen

Mr. Vanderbilt's bedroom

Third Floor

The third floor contains eight bedrooms and a sitting room decorated in Louis XVI style walnut paneling by Ogden Codman. The North Wing of the third floor quarters were reserved for domestic servants. With ceilings near 18 feet high, Richard Morris Hunt created two separate third floors to allow a mass congregation of servant bed chambers. This was all in part of the configuration of the house, built in Italian Renaissance style, that called for a pitched roof. Flat roofed French classical houses in the area allowed a concealed wing for staffing at the time. The Breakers does not feature this luxury.

A total of 30 bedrooms are located in the two third floor staff quarters. Three additional bedrooms for the Butler, Chef, and Visiting Valet are located on the Mezzanine "Entrasol" Floor located between the first and second floor just to the rear of the main kitchen.

Attic Floor

The Attic floor contained more staff quarters, general storage areas, and the innovative cisterns. One smaller cistern supplied hydraulic pressure for the 1895 Otis lift, still functioning in the house though wired for electricity in 1933. Two larger cisterns supplied fresh and salt water to the many bathrooms in the house.

Over the Grand Staircase sits a stained glass skylight designed by artist John La Farge. Originally built in the Vanderbilt's 1 West 57th Street townhouse dining room, the skylight was removed in 1894 during an expansion of the house.

The Architect

The Breakers is also a definitive expression of Beaux-Arts architecture in American domestic design by one of the country's founding fathers of architecture, Richard Morris Hunt. The Breakers is one of the few surviving works of Hunt that has not been demolished in the last century and is therefore valuable for its rarity as well as its architectural excellence. The Breakers was Hunt's final work, and is the singular house that has withstood the vagaries of time to be remembered as the monument that was the architect's greatest achievement. The Breakers made Hunt the "dean of American architecture" as well as helping define the era in American life which Hunt helped to shape.

Materials

- Foundation: Brick, Concrete and Limestone
- Trusses: Steel
- Walls: Indiana Limestone
- Roof: Terra cotta Red Tile
- Wall Panels: Platinum leaf
- Other: marble (plaques), wrought iron (gates & fences)

See also

- Largest Historic Homes in the United States

Further reading

- Wilson, Richard Guy, Diane Pilgrim, and Richard N. Murray. American Renaissance 1876–1917. New York: The Brooklyn Museum, 1979.
- Baker, Paul R. Richard Morris Hunt. Cambridge, MA: The MIT Press, 1980.
- Benway, Ann. A Guidebook to Newport Mansions. Preservation Society of Newport County, 1984.

- Croffut, William A. The Vanderbilts and the Story of their Fortune. Chicago and New York: Belford, Clarke and Company, 1886.
- Downing, Antoinette F. and Vincent J. Scully, Jr. The Architectural Heritage of Newport, Rhode Island. 2nd edition, New York: Clarkson N. Potter, Inc., 1967.
- Ferree, Barr. American Estates and Gardens. New York: Munn and Company, 1904.
- Gannon, Thomas. Newport Mansions: the Gilded Age. Fort Church Publishers, Inc., 1982.
- Jordy, William H., and Christopher P. Monkhouse. Buildings on Paper: Brown University, Rhode Island Historical Society and Rhode Island School of Design, 1982.
- Lints, Eric P. "The Breakers: A Construction and Technologies Report" Newport, RI: The Newport Preservation Society of Newport County, 1992.
- Metcalf, Pauline C., ed. Ogden Codman and the Decoration of Houses. Boston: The Boston Athenaeum, 1988.
- Patterson, Jerry E. The Vanderbilts. New York: Harry N. Abrams, Inc., 1989.
- Perschler, Martin. "Historic Landscapes Project" Newport, RI: The Preservation Society of Newport County, 1993.
- Schuyler, Montgomery. "The Works of the Late Richard M. Hunt," The Architectural Record, Vol. V., October–December, 1895: p. 180.
- Smales, Holbert T. "The Breakers" Newport, Rhode Island. Newport, RI: Remington Ward, 1951.
- Thorndike, Joseph J., ed. Three Centuries of Notable American Architects. New York: American Heritage Publishing Co., Inc., 1981.

External links

- Official Site [1]
- Complete details of the building, from the United States Department of the Interior, National Park Service [2] (Adobe PDF file)

Marble House

For the Knife song, see Marble House (song). For other uses see Marble House (disambiguation)

Marble House	
U.S. National Register of Historic Places	
U.S. National Historic Landmark	
Marble House's entrance ramp allows vehicles to drive in from Bellevue Avenue on one side and exit on the other	
Location:	Newport, RI
Coordinates:	41°27′43.04″N 71°18′20.22″W
Built/Founded:	1892
Architect:	Richard Morris Hunt
Architectural style(s):	Beaux Arts
Governing body:	Newport Historical Society
Added to NRHP:	September 10, 1971
Designated NHL:	February 17, 1976
NRHP Reference#:	71000025

Marble House is one of the Gilded Age mansions of Newport, Rhode Island, now open to the public as a museum. It was designed by the architect Richard Morris Hunt, and said to be inspired by the Petit Trianon at Versailles (which it resembles in little more than pilasters and balustrades). Grounds were designed by noted landscape architect Ernest W. Bowditch. Marble House was built between 1888 and 1892 for William Kissam Vanderbilt, grandson of Commodore Cornelius Vanderbilt. The house was a social landmark that helped spark the transformation of Newport from a relatively relaxed summer colony of wooden houses to the now legendary resort of opulent stone palaces. It was reported to cost $11 million ($260000000 in 2009 dollars) of which $7 million was spent on 500,000 cubic feet (14,000 m³) of marble. Upon its completion, Mr. Vanderbilt gave the house to his wife Alva Erskine Smith as her 39th birthday present. William Vanderbilt's older brother Cornelius Vanderbilt II subsequently built the grandest of Newport cottages, The Breakers, between 1893 and 1895.

The Chinese Tea House at the Sea

Rear view of mansion facing sea, 1968

After the Vanderbilts divorced in 1895, Alva married Oliver Hazard Perry Belmont, moving down the street to Belcourt. After his death, she reopened Marble House and added a Chinese Tea House on its seaside cliffs, where she hosted rallies for women's suffrage. She sold the house to Frederick H. Prince in 1932. Prince's estate gave the house and its furnishings to the Preservation Society of Newport County in 1963.

In 1971 it was added to the National Register of Historic Places. Five years later the Department of the Interior designated it, and the Bellevue Avenue Historic District in which it is located, as National Historic Landmarks.

Additionally, The Great Gatsby (1974 film) and True Lies were filmed here.

References

- Hopf, John T. (1976). *The Complete Book of Newport Mansions.*

External links

- Marble House [1]

Newport Tower (Rhode Island)

Newport Tower	
 The Newport Tower.	
Origin	
Mill name	Newport Tower
Mill location	Newport, Rhode Island. 41°29′08″N 71°18′35″W
Year built	Mid C17th
Information	
Purpose	Corn mill
Type	Tower mill

The **Newport Tower** (also known as: **Round Tower**, **Touro Tower**, **Newport Stone Tower**, **Old Stone Mill**, **OSM** and **Mystery Tower**) is a round stone tower located in Touro Park in Newport, Rhode Island (USA).

It is commonly considered to have been a windmill built in the mid 17th century. However, the tower has received attention due to speculation that it is actually several centuries older and represents evidence of pre-Columbian trans-oceanic contact.

Description

The Newport Tower is located in Touro Park, at the top of Mill Street, surrounded by a historical residential neighborhood on the hill above the waterfront tourist district. Eighteenth-century paintings show that the hill itself once furnished a view of the harbor and would have been visible to passing mariners in Narragansett Bay, but recent tree growth now obscures the view of the harbor from the top of the tower.

The Newport Tower is not exactly circular. From southeast to northwest the diameter reportedly measures 22 feet 2 inches, but when measured from east to west, the diameter lengthens to 23 feet

3 inches, although curiously, 19th century measurements of the interior gave an east-west dimension of 18 feet 4 inches, which was slightly shorter than the north-south measurement of 18 feet 9 inches, suggesting that the discrepancies may be due to the unevenness of the rubble masonry. The tower has a height of 28 feet and an exterior width of 24 feet. At one time the sides were coated with a smooth coating of white plaster, the remains of which can still be seen clinging to the outer walls. It is supported by eight cylindrical columns that form stone arches, two of which are slightly broader than the other six. Above the arches and inside the tower is evidence of a floor that once supported an interior chamber. The walls are approximately 3 feet thick, and the diameter of the inner chamber is approximately 18 feet. The chamber is penetrated by four windows on what used to be the main floor, and three very small ones at the upper level. Almost (but not quite directly) opposite the west window is a fireplace backed with grey stone and flanked by nooks.

A representation of the tower is featured prominently on the Seal and unit patch of the former US Navy vessel, USS *Newport*.

In a document of 1741 the tower is described as "the old stone mill." In 1760 the Tower was used as a haymow, while in 1767 it was described as having been used as a powder store "some time past". De Barres' plan of Newport, published in 1776, marks it as "Stone Wind Mill." During the American Revolution, the tower was used by the Americans as a lookout, and by the British to store munitions. A painting of the tower circa 1777 is here: [1]

Nothing in early Norse architecture is similar, in size or appearance, to the Newport Tower. However, this 17th Century windmill near Chesterton, England, shares many characteristics with the Newport Tower

Construction

The tower is located at the upper end of the plot behind the now-demolished mansion built by Benedict Arnold, the first colonial governor of Rhode Island, who moved from Pawtuxet to Newport in 1651 (not to be confused with his great-grandson, General Benedict Arnold of the American Revolutionary War.) In 1677 Arnold mentions "my stone built Wind Mill" in his will: the site for his then-new burying-ground, which survives to this day, is between this mill and his mansion. The phrase has therefore generally been accepted as referring to the Newport Tower, and is evidence the tower was once used as a windmill.

An illustration from the British "Penny Magazine", published in 1836 (shown at right), revealed to the Americans that the tower is of a similar type to Chesterton Windmill, a 17th century mill near Chesterton, Warwickshire, England. The notion that Arnold was born in Leamington, Warwickshire, only a few miles from Chesterton, is mistaken: the family lived near Limington in Somerset, about 100 miles away. However, Chesterton windmill stands on a ridge within half a mile of one of the main southwest–northeast roads of early modern Britain, which also runs past Limington, and it is entirely plausible that Arnold, or another colonist in a position to influence the design of his "stone built windmill", would have seen it. One such candidate is George Lawton, who was born in 1607 about 30 km from Chesterton and is thought to have built several mills in the area. 'Georg Lawtons Mill' is mentioned in a 1668 document as being on the current Newport Mill Street.

Scientific investigations

1848 mortar comparison

In 1848, the Rev. Dr. Jackson of Newport collected samples of mortar from the mill and some of the oldest known structures in the town, including the very early Bull house (c1640), the Easton house (1642-3), other houses, and the tombs of Governor Arnold and his wife. Under detailed examination, all proved to be of very similar composition, "composed of shell lime, sand, and gravel".

1948 excavation

The city of Newport gave permission for a scientific investigation of the site by the Society for American Archaeology in 1948. The investigation was directed by Hugh Henken of Harvard University, with the field work headed by William S. Godfrey. As part of the investigation, a one-meter wide trench was dug from the tower's exterior through the interior. The results, published in Godfrey's 1951 Ph.D. dissertation, concluded that all the artifacts discovered were from the 17th century. Godfrey's dissertation identifies Benedict Arnold as the builder of the tower, stating that Arnold "purchased some of his Newport property, specifically the section on which he later built his house and the stone mill, the year before he moved... At some period before 1677 Arnold built the Old Stone Mill."

Godfrey initially dismissed the Chesterton Mill theory, claiming that "On the other hand, there is very little probability that Benedict built his Tower as a mill... the tower mill form, as contrasted to the smock, post and composite forms, was not common in England until the beginning of the 18th century." Godfrey posited the hypothesis that "the tower was built as a comfortable retreat and lookout for a very rich and very autocratic old man." However, he later retreated from this position, noting in 1954 that "Rex Wailes, noted English expert on windmills,... has supported the contention that both structures were built as mills." It has since been shown that tower mills were known in England from the late thirteenth century and that they became increasingly common from the late sixteenth century onwards. Subsequent research has determined that Chesterton was, in fact, built as a windmill in 1632-3, as the original building accounts, including payments for sailcloths, having been traced since Wailes' death in 1986. There are also several surviving seventeenth century stone tower mills in North

America, which are similar in appearance to European examples of the same period (e.g. Moulin de Grondines, Quebec (1674) and Moulin de Vincelotte, Quebec (1690)).

1992 carbon-14 dating

In 1992, radiocarbon dating tests of the tower's mortar were undertaken by a team of researchers from Denmark and Finland. The results suggest a probable date of construction between 1635 and 1698.

2006–2008 excavations

In October and November 2006 and again in October and November 2007, the Chronognostic Research Foundation provided the funds necessary to conduct an archaeological investigation of the anomalies discovered in Touro Park during geophysical studies of the past three years. These anomalies were tested in the excavation plan created by the cultural resource management firm Gray and Pape. Multiple levels of fill and the existence of earlier gravel paths from various decades in the 19th and 20th centuries were uncovered. While no artifacts or deposits relating to the building of the tower were found during these excavations, the project uncovered numerous interesting aspects of the park during its existence, especially the change in landscape and what sorts of events were transpiring there. These were the first archaeological excavations to take place in Touro Park in nearly 60 years. The primary goal of this research project was to answer the question: Who built the Newport Tower? Press reports following the first digging season clearly show that the earliest date of any one of the many artifacts excavated was 17th century.

At the end of the second digging season, in November 2007, Janet Barstad, president of the Chronognostic Foundation, surprised Newport city councilors by refocusing attention on the astronomical alignments (discussed below) as evidence for a medieval date of construction, on the basis that the archaeological excavations had not found anything conclusively related to the tower.

Informed by the city authorities in spring 2008 that the asphalt path around the tower was to be removed and replaced with concrete, Chronognostic arranged for some of their experienced local volunteers to undertake several small excavations after the old path material had been removed, lasting from May 30 to June 4. They concentrated on areas directly in line with the Tower pillars, and in two of the three major pits they dug, found columns of discoloration, about 35 cm in diameter, which appeared to indicate the former presence of substantial wooden posts about 4 metres out from the tower walls, possibly supports for a wooden roof. No such discoloration was found in the third aligned test pit, or in a smaller pit dug without reference to the Tower columns. Small finds included charcoal, but carbon dating of this was inconclusive.

Alternative hypotheses

Despite there being no archaeological artifacts nor documents which would date the Tower to the pre-Colonial period, several writers have advanced ideas about the tower's origin apart from the now mainstream windmill theory.

Norse

In 1837 the Danish archaeologist Carl Christian Rafn in his book *Antiquitates Americanæ*, partly based on his research of the inscriptions on the Dighton Rock near the mouth of the Taunton River, proposed a Viking origin for the tower. This hypothesis is predicated on the uncertainty of the southward extent of the early Norse explorations of North America, particularly in regard to the actual location of Vinland. Rafn's popularization of the theory led to a flurry of interest

The Newport Tower, *circa* 1894

and "proofs" of Norse settlement in the area. Henry Wadsworth Longfellow incorporated the Norse-origin view of the tower into his poem "The Skeleton in Armor". Phillip Ainsworth Means, an archaeologist whose speciality was Latin America, attempted to compile all known evidence surrounding the tower to date in his 1942 book *The Newport Tower*. As a supporter of the Norse hypothesis, Means dismissed the idea that Arnold built the tower "from the ground up."

Since then much of Means' evidence has been shown to be mistaken. Means' assertion that a windmill would not have fireplaces because of the fire risk is incorrect. Several have fireplaces aligned with windows and it is not unusual to find a double flue exiting out of the wall, generally with the exits aligned parallel to the prevailing wind to improve the updraft on a relatively short flue (e.g. Upholland Windmill, Lancashire, where the fireplace is at second floor (Br Eng = First floor) level, and the doors and windows are aligned to the cardinal points of the compass; or Much Wenlock windmill, Shropshire, which has double flues of uncertain purpose rising from the middle floor level. A conventional chimney could not be used as it would foul the turning cap and sails of the windmill.

Observatory hypothesis

Four of the eight supporting pillars of the tower face the main points of the compass, although other aspects of the design seem curiously haphazard. In the 1990s, William Penhallow, an astronomer at the University of Rhode Island, studied the windows in the tower and said that he found a number of astronomical alignments. At the summer solstice the setting sun should shine through the "west" window (actually just south of true west) onto a niche in the inner wall, next to the "south" window. (This no longer happens due to urban development and park trees.) Similarly, the angle from the "east" window through the "west" window is about 18 degrees south of west, which is the southern extreme of moonsets during what is known as the "lunar minor standstill". The smaller windows also form alignments, on significant stars. These alignments could be accidental, but if they were deliberate it would explain why the pattern of windows seems, according to Penhallow, "so odd".

Chinese

The author Gavin Menzies argues in *1421: The Year China Discovered America* that the tower was built by a colony of Chinese sailors and concubines from the junks of Zheng He's voyages either as a lighthouse, or, based on Penhallow's findings, as an observatory to determine the longitude of the colony. Menzies claimed that the tower closely matches designs used in Chinese observatories and lighthouses elsewhere. However, these claims have been debunked.

Portuguese

During the early 20th century, Edmund B. Delabarre associated the Dighton Rock with the lost Portuguese navigators Miguel Corte-Real and his brother Gaspar. This Portuguese hypothesis has been supported more recently by Manuel Luciano DaSilva, who suggests that one of the Corte-Real brothers built the Newport Tower as a watchtower. The idea of Portuguese construction of the tower was also supported by former U.S. Ambassador Herbert Pell, who in 1948 argued that the tower resembles elements of the Convent of Tomar in Portugal.

Medieval Templars

The prolific British writer Andrew Sinclair has put forth the hypothesis that the Newport Tower was built by medieval Scottish Templars led by the Scottish earl Henry Sinclair, as part of an alleged voyage to New England about a hundred years before Columbus. Sinclair's alleged voyage to America also appeared in the international best-seller Holy Blood Holy Grail, but this claim has been vigorously disputed.

See also

Oldest buildings in the United States

External links

- Redwood Library site on Newport Tower [2]
- "The Newport Tower and the Plowden Petition" article from *Skeptical Intelligencer* [3]

Touro Synagogue

Touro Synagogue National Historic Site

Location	Newport, Rhode Island, USA
Coordinates	41°29′22″N 71°18′43″W
Area	0.23 acre (930 m²)
Established	March 5, 1946
Governing body	Touro Synagogue Foundation

The **Touro Synagogue** is a 1763 synagogue in Newport, Rhode Island, that is the oldest synagogue building still standing in the United States, the oldest surviving Jewish synagogue building in North America and the only surviving synagogue building in the U.S. dating to the colonial era.

History

It was designed by noted British-Colonial era architect and Rhode Island resident Peter Harrison and is considered his most notable work. The interior is flanked by a series of twelve Ionic columns supporting balconies. The columns signify the twelve tribes of ancient Israel. Each column is carved from a single tree. Located at 85 Touro Street, the Touro Synagogue remains an active Orthodox synagogue. The building is oriented to face east toward Jerusalem. The ark containing the Torah is on the east wall; above it is a mural representing the Ten Commandments in Hebrew. It was painted by the Newport artist Benjamin Howland.

Touro Synagogue, America's oldest
surviving synagogue building

The Touro Synagogue was built from 1759 to 1763 for the Jeshuat Israel congregation in Newport under the leadership of Cantor (Chazzan) Isaac Touro. The cornerstone was laid by Aaron Lopez, a prominent merchant in Newport involved in the spermaceti candlemaking business and other commercial ventures. The Jeshuat Israel congregation itself dates back to 1658 when fifteen Spanish and Portuguese Jewish families arrived, probably from the West Indies, and many settled near Easton's Point.[1] The synagogue was formally dedicated 2 December 1763. Other notable leaders include Abraham Pereira Mendes and Henry Samuel Morais (1900–01).

In 1790, the synagogue's warden, Moses Seixas, wrote to George Washington, expressing his support for Washington's administration and good wishes for him. Washington sent a letter in response, which read in part:

> ...the Government of the United States...gives to bigotry no sanction, to persecution no assistance...May the children of the Stock of Abraham, who dwell in this land, continue to merit and enjoy the good will of the other Inhabitants; while every one shall sit in safety under his own vine and figtree, and there shall be none to make him afraid. May the father of all mercies scatter light and not darkness in our paths, and make us all in our several vocations useful here, and in his own due time and way everlastingly happy."

Judah Touro, the son of Isaac Touro and his wife Reyna, made a fortune as a merchant in New Orleans. He left $10,000 in his will for the upkeep of the Jewish cemetery and synagogue in Newport.

A legend exists that the trap door under the *tebáh* (bimah) was used while the synagogue was a stop on the Underground Railroad. This is unfounded.

In 1946, Touro Synagogue was designated a National Historic Site and is an affiliated area of the National Park Service. The synagogue was listed on the National Register of Historic Places on October 15, 1966. In 2001, the congregation joined into a partnership with the National Trust for Historic Preservation.

Congregation

The congregation at Newport, never large, was composed of Jews with roots in the Sephardic Spanish and Portuguese diaspora, with some Ashkenazim by the eighteenth century.

The first Jewish residents of Newport, fifteen Spanish Jewish families, arrived in 1658. It is presumed that they arrived via the community in Curaçao. The small community worshipped in rooms in private homes for more than a century before they could afford to build a synagogue.

The community purchased and dedicated the Jewish Cemetery at Newport in 1677.

The city of Newport faded in importance shortly after American independence, after the capital of Rhode Island moved to Providence, which rapidly also surpassed Newport as a seaport. The Jewish community, too small to maintain a synagogue, removed the Torah scrolls and sent them for safekeeping along with the deed to the building to Congregation Shearith Israel in New York. It still formally owns the Touro synagogue. The keys left the Jewish community and were passed to the Goulds, a Quaker family in Newport.

From the 1850s on, the building was occasionally opened for worship for the convenience of summer visitors. It was reopened on a regular basis in 1883 as Jewish life in Newport revived with the late nineteenth century immigration of eastern European Jews. The synagogue acquired a nearby building and ran a Hebrew School and other activities. In the late twentieth century, the number of Jews in Newport dwindled again. The synagogue has had a special relationship with Jewish naval families stationed in Newport. It continues to serve a small congregation, supplemented by travelers who spend the Sabbath in Newport.

Images

synagogue side view in 2008

See also

- Touro Cemetery
- Touro Synagogue (New Orleans)
- Partners for Sacred Places
- Oldest synagogues in the United States

External links

- Touro Synagogue [2] (Official website)
- Loeb Visitors Center at Touro Synagogue [3] (Official website)
- Touro Synagogue National Historic Site [4] (National Park Service profile)
- News on Touro Synagogue [5]
- Washington's and Seixas' letters
- 2005-2006 Restoration [6]

Newport Casino

Newport Casino	
U.S. National Register of Historic Places	
U.S. National Historic Landmark	
Casino facade in 2008	
Location:	Newport, Rhode Island
Coordinates:	41°28′56″N 71°18′27″W
Built/Founded:	1879
Architect:	McKim, Mead & White
Architectural style(s):	Shingle Style
Governing body:	Private
Added to NRHP:	December 2, 1970
Designated NHL:	February 27, 1987
NRHP Reference#:	70000083

The **Newport Casino** is located at 186-202 Bellevue Avenue, Newport, Rhode Island, United States. It was designated a National Historic Landmark on February 27, 1987.

History (1879 - 1900)

The complex was commissioned in 1880 by James Gordon Bennett, Jr. Legend states that Bennett placed a bet with his guest British Cavalry Officer, Captain Henry Augustus "Sugar" Candy that Candy would not ride his horse up onto the front porch of Newport's most exclusive men's club - The Newport Reading Room. Candy won the bet, but the Governors of the Reading Room were not amused. Bennett and his infamous short temper did not take this kindly, and soon set about creating his own retreat, what would eventually become The Newport Casino.

Soon after deciding to create his own social club, Bennett purchased the Sidney Brooks estate, "Stone Villa" [1]. Directly across the street was a vacant lot, suitable for construction of the Casino. Bennett hired Charles McKim (soon to be of the firm McKim, Mead, and White) to design the Casino. By January 1880, Nathan Barker of Newport, RI, was contracted to begin construction.

The interior of the Casino, while generally outlined by McKim, was entrusted to Stanford White. Taking many elements and cues from the Japanese Pavilion at the 1876 Centennial International Exhibition in Philadelphia, White provided for a plan that was both secluded and open.

The Newport Casino opened to its first patrons in July 1880, and the general public got their first view in August 1880.

History (1900 - 1954)

The first half of the 20th century was unkind to the Newport Casino. The Gilded age drew to a close with the onset of the Depression, and the Newport fell by the wayside as a summer resort for the wealthy and powerful. The Casino struggled financially as a social club right from the start, and by the 1950s the Casino was in sad shape. Like many of the mansions, there was the very real possibility that it would be demolished to make way for more modern retail space.

Tennis, however, would be its saving grace. Having always had a sporting flair, the United States Lawn Tennis Association held their first championships at the Casino in 1881, an event that would continue through 1914. By this time, tennis was firmly entrenched as the key attraction at the Casino.

Fortunately, Jimmy and Candy Van Alen stepped in, and by 1954 had established the Tennis Hall of Fame and Museum in the Newport Casino. The combination of prominent headliners at the tennis matches and the museum allowed the building to be saved.

It stands today as one of the finest examples of Victorian Shingle Style architecture in the world. The buildings are generally well preserved, and the Casino Theatre which was in bad condition is being restored.

The landscaping in the center, new bushes were recently put in the entrance way with the old overgrown bushes removed.

Buildings

The complex includes:

- The Casino (shops, a restaurant, offices, and the International Tennis Hall of Fame)
- Horseshoe Piazza and Court
- Bill Talbert Stadium
- Court Tennis Building (The National Court Tennis Club) [2]
- Theatre (now being restored)
- Indoor tennis courts (Newport Casino Indoor Racquet Club) [3]
- Various grass tennis courts (Newport Casino Lawn Tennis Club) [4]

Sports

The Newport Casino was never a public gambling establishment. Originally, "casino" meant a small villa built for pleasure. During the 19th century, the term casino came to include other buildings where social activities took place.

In its heyday during the Gilded Age, the Newport Casino offered a wide array of social diversions to the summer colony including archery, billiards, bowling, concerts, dancing, dining, horse shows, lawn bowling, reading, real tennis, tea parties, and theatricals. It was best known as the home of American lawn tennis; the Casino hosted the 1881–1914 National Championships, later called the U.S. Open.

Today, there is still an active grass-court tennis club, as well as an indoor tennis club. The Newport Casino Croquet Club offers championship croquet play on Newport's grass courts.

The Court Tennis Building is part of the original complex, built in 1880. It burned down in 1945, but was rebuilt in 1980. It is home to the National Tennis Club.

External links

- Newport Casino, 186-202 Bellevue Avenue, Newport, Newport County, RI: 21 photos, 21 data pages [5], at Historic American Building Survey
- Description of the Casino Theatre [6]
- Official site of the International Tennis Hall of Fame [7]

International Tennis Hall of Fame

The **International Tennis Hall of Fame** is a non-profit tennis hall of fame and museum at the Newport Casino in Newport, Rhode Island, USA. The organization honors the greatest players and contributors of the game and offers tennis fans a remarkable tennis landmark, featuring an extensive museum, grass tennis courts, an indoor tennis facility, and a court tennis (or real tennis) facility.

History

The International Tennis Hall of Fame & Museum is located at by the Newport Casino. The complex was commissioned in 1880 by James Gordon Bennett, Jr. Legend has it that Bennett placed a bet with his guest British Cavalry Officer, Captain Henry Augustus "Sugar" Candy that Candy would not ride his horse up onto the front porch of Newport's most exclusive men's club - The Reading Room. Candy won the bet, but the Governors of the Reading Room were not amused. Bennett and his infamous short temper did not take this kindly, and soon set about creating his own retreat, what would eventually become The Newport Casino.

The Newport Casino, home to the hall of fame

The first half of the 20th century was unkind to the Newport Casino. The Gilded age drew to a close with the onset of the Depression, and the Newport fell by the wayside as a summer resort for the wealthy and powerful. The Casino struggled financially as a social club right from the start, and by the 1950s the Casino was in sad shape. Like many of the mansions, there was the very real possibility that it would be demolished to make way for more modern retail space.

Tennis, however, would be its saving grace. Having always had a sporting flair, the United State Lawn Tennis Association held their first championships at the Casino in 1881, an event that would continue through 1914. By this time, tennis was firmly entrenched as the key attraction at the Casino.

Fortunately, James Van Alen stepped in, and by 1954 had established the Tennis Hall of Fame and Museum in the Newport Casino. The combination of prominent headliners at the tennis matches and the museum allowed the building to be saved.

It stands today as one of the finest examples of Victorian Shingle Style architecture in the world. The buildings are generally well preserved, except for the Casino Theatre which is in poor condition.

The International Tennis Hall of Fame was founded in 1954 by James Van Alen as "a shrine to the ideals of the game". He was elected president of the hall in 1957. The International Tennis Hall of

Fame is one of the largest and finest tennis museums in the world. The International Tennis Hall of Fame was officially sanctioned by the United States Tennis Association in 1954 and recognized by the International Tennis Federation in 1986. The first Hall of Fame members were inducted in 1955; as of 2010, there are 218 inductees from 19 countries.

Collection

The museum houses a vast collection of artifacts and memorabilia (including videos, photographs, audio recordings, tennis equipment and apparel, trophies, and art) highlighting the history of tennis from its origins up through the modern era. The collection is displayed year-round in the museum's 13000 square feet (1200 m^2) of exhibit space.

Tournaments

The Hall of Fame hosts several tournaments, including:

July 4–10, 2011: Campbell's Hall of Fame Tennis Championships

Part of the ATP World Tour, the tournament is one of 15 events and the only grass court event in North America. Top male players come to Newport direct from Wimbledon to compete for the Van Alen Cup and $442,500 in prize money at the International Tennis Hall of Fame. Past competitors include Americans Sam Querrey and Mardy Fish, as well as two-time champion Fabrice Santoro of France.

July 10: Hall of Fame Induction Ceremony

The Class of 2011 will take their place in the International Tennis Hall of Fame on Saturday, July 11. The inductees will be announced in February 2011. Andre Agassi, former world No. 1, eight-time Grand Slam champion, and two-time Olympic gold medalist headlines the ballot for induction. Agassi is the sole nominee in the Recent Player Category. Joining Agassi on the ballot in the Master Player Category are Thelma Coyne Long, who dominated Australian tennis in the 1930s -1950s, and Christine Truman Janes, a British star of the 1950s and 1960s. Nominated in the Contributor Category are influential tennis promoter and administrator Mike Davies and Fern Lee "Peachy" Kellmeyer, who has played a vital role in the growth of women's tennis.

Members

Contributor category

Name	Life span	Nationality	Year inducted
Adams, Russ	1930–	United States	2007
Adee, George	1874–1948	United States	1964
Baker, Lawrence	1890–1980	United States	1975
Chatrier, Philippe	1926–2003	France	1992
Clerici, Gianni	1930–	Italy	2006
Collins, Arthur "Bud"	1929–	United States	1994
Cullman III, Joseph	1912–2004	United States	1990
Danzig, Allison	1898–1987	United States	1968
David, Herman	1905–1974	Great Britain	1998
Dell, Donald	1937–	United States	2009
Gray, David	1927–1983	Great Britain	1985
Griffin, Clarence	1888–1973	United States	1970
Gustav V of Sweden	1858–1950	Sweden	1980
Hardwick, Derek	1921–1987	Great Britain	2010
Heldman, Gladys	1922–2003	United States	1979
Hester, William	1912–1993	United States	1981
Hunt, Lamar	1932–2006	United States	1993
Schultz, Alexander	1926–2003	United States	1992
Johnson, Robert	1899–1971	United States	2009
Jones, Perry	1890–1970	United States	1970
Kelleher, Robert	1913–	United States	2000
Laney, Al	1895–1988	United States	1979
McCormack, Mark	1930–2003	United States	2008
Myrick, Julian	1880–1969	United States	1963
Nielsen, Arthur	1923–1980	United States	1971
Outerbridge, Mary	1852–1886	United States	1979
Parks, Brad		United States	2010

Scott, Eugene	1937–2006	United States	2008
Tinling, Ted	1910–2000	Great Britain	1986
Tobin, Brian	1930–	Australia	2003
Van Alen, James	1902–1991	United States	1965
Wingfield, Walter Clopton	1833–1912	Great Britain	1997

Player category

Name	Nationality	Year inducted
Addie, Pauline Betz	United States	1965
Alexander, Frederick "Fred"	United States	1961
Allison, Wilmer	United States	1963
Alonso, Manuel	Spain	1977
Anderson, Malcolm	Australia	2000
Ashe, Arthur	United States	1985
Atkinson, Juliette	United States	1974
Austin, Henry	Great Britain	1997
Austin, Tracy	United States	1992
Barrett, Angela Mortimer	Great Britain	1993
Becker, Boris	Germany	2003
Behr, Karl	United States	1969
Borg, Björn	Sweden	1987
Borotra, Jean	France	1976
Bowrey, Lesley Turner	Australia	1997
Brinker, Maureen Connolly	United States	1968
Bromwich, John	Australia	1984
Brookes, Norman	Australia	1977
Browne, Mary Kendall	United States	1957
Brugnon, Jacques	France	1976
Buchholz Jr., Earl	United States	2005
Budge, John Donald "Don"	United States	1964

Bueno, Maria	Brazil	1978
Bundy, May Sutton	United States	1956
Cahill, Mabel	Ireland	1976
Campbell, Oliver	United States	1955
Casals, Rosemary	United States	1996
Cawley, Evonne Goolagong	Australia	1988
Chace, Malcolm	United States	1961
Chambers, Dorothea Douglass Lambert	Great Britain	1981
Chang, Michael	United States	2008
Cheney, Dorothy Bundy	United States	2004
Clapp, Louise Brough	United States	1967
Clark, Clarence	United States	1983
Clark, Joseph	United States	1955
Clothier, William	United States	1956
Cochet, Henri	France	1976
Connors, James "Jimmy"	United States	1998
Cooke, Sarah Palfrey	United States	1963
Cooper, Ashley	Australia	1991
Courier, Jim	United States	2005
Court, Margaret	Australia	1979
Crawford, Jack	Australia	1979
Davidson, Owen	Australia	2010
Davidson, Sven	Sweden	2007
Davis, Dwight F.	United States	1956
Dod, Charlotte "Lottie"	Great Britain	1983
Doeg, John	United States	1962
Doherty, Lawrence	Great Britain	1980
Doherty, Reggie	Great Britain	1980
Drobný, Jaroslav	Czech Republic	1983
duPont, Margaret Osborne	United States	1967
Dwight, James	United States	1955

Durr, Françoise	France	2003
Edberg, Stefan	Sweden	2004
Emerson, Roy	Australia	1982
Etchebaster, Pierre	France	1978
Evert, Christine "Chris"	United States	1995
Falkenburg, Robert "Bob"	United States/Brazil	1974
Fernández, Beatriz "Gigi"	United States (Puerto Rico)	2010
Fraser, Neale	Australia	1984
Garland, Chuck	United States	1969
Gibson, Althea	United States	1971
Gimeno, Andres	Spain	2009
Godfree, Kathleen McKane	Great Britain	1978
Gonzalez, Pancho	United States	1968
Graf, Stefanie "Steffi"	Germany	2004
Grant, Bitsy	United States	1972
Hackett, Harold	United States	1961
Hansell, Ellen	United States	1965
Hard, Darlene	United States	1973
Hart, Doris	United States	1969
Hewitt, Robert "Bob"	Australia/South Africa	1992
Hoad, Lewis "Lew"	Australia	1980
Hopman, Harry	Australia	1978
Hovey, Frederick	United States	1974
Hunt, Joseph "Joe"	United States	1966
Hunter, Frank	United States	1961
Irvin, Shirley Fry	United States	1970
Jacobs, Helen	United States	1962
Johnston, William "Bill"	United States	1958
Jones, Ann Haydon	Great Britain	1985
King, Billie Jean Moffitt	United States	1987
Kodeš, Jan	Czechoslovakia	1990
Koželuh, Karel	Czechoslovakia	2006

Kramer, John Albert "Jack"	United States	1968
Lacoste, René	France	1976
Larned, William "Bill"	United States	1956
Larsen, Arthur "Art"	United States	1956
Laver, Rodney "Rod"	Australia	1981
Lendl, Ivan	Czechoslovakia/United States	2001
Lenglen, Suzanne	France	1978
Little, Dorothy Round	Great Britain	1986
Lott, George	United States	1964
Macdonald, Andrew	Great Britain	1987
Mako, Constantine "Gene"	United States	1973
Mallory, Molla	Norway/United States	1958
Mandlíková, Hana	Czechoslovakia/Australia	1994
Marble, Alice	United States	1964
Martin, Alastair	United States	1973
Martin, William McChesney	United States	1982
Maskell, Dan	Great Britain	1996
McEnroe, John	United States	1999
McGregor, Kenneth "Ken"	Australia	1999
McKinley, Charles Robert "Chuck"	United States	1986
McLoughlin, Maurice	United States	1957
McMillan, Frew	South Africa	1992
McNeill, Don	United States	1965
Moody, Helen Wills	United States	1969
Moore, Elisabeth	United States	1971
Mulloy, Gardnar	United States	1972
Murray, Robert	United States	1958
Năstase, Ilie	Romania	1991
Navrátilová, Martina	Czechoslovakia/United States	2000
Newcombe, John	Australia	1986
Noah, Yannick	France	2005
Novotná, Jana	Czech Republic	2005

Nüsslein, Hans	Germany	2006
Nuthall, Betty	Great Britain	1977
Olmedo, Alex	Peru/United States	1987
Osuna, Rafael	Mexico	1979
Parker, Frank	United States	1966
Patterson, Gerald	Australia	1989
Patty, Jesse "Budge"	United States	1977
Pell, Theodore	United States	1966
Perry, Frederick "Fred"	Great Britain	1975
Pettitt, Tom	Great Britain	1982
Pietrangeli, Nicola	Italy	1986
Quist, Adrian	Australia	1984
Rafter, Patrick "Pat"	Australia	2006
Ralston, Dennis	United States	1987
Renshaw, Ernest	Great Britain	1983
Renshaw, William	Great Britain	1983
Richards, Vincent	United States	1961
Richey, Nancy	United States	2003
Riggs, Robert "Bobby"	United States	1967
Roche, Anthony "Tony"	Australia	1986
Roosevelt, Ellen	United States	1975
Rose, Mervyn	Australia	2001
Rosewall, Kenneth "Ken"	Australia	1980
Ryan, Elizabeth	United States	1972
Sabatini, Gabriela	Argentina	2006
Sampras, Pete	United States	2007
Santana, Manuel	Spain	1985
Savitt, Richard "Dick"	United States	1976
Schroeder, Frederick "Ted"	United States	1966
Sears, Eleonora	United States	1968
Sears, Richard	United States	1955
Sedgman, Frank	Australia	1979

Segura, Pancho	Ecuador	1984
Seixas, Elias Victor "Vic"	United States	1971
Seles, Monica	Yugoslavia/United States	2009
Shriver, Pamela "Pam"	United States	2002
Shields, Frank	United States	1964
Slocum, Henry	United States	1955
Smith, Stanley "Stan"	United States	1987
Stolle, Frederick "Fred"	Australia	1985
Talbert, William "Bill"	United States	1967
Tilden, William "Bill"	United States	1959
Tingay, Lance	Great Britain	1982
Townsend, Bertha Toulmin	United States	1974
Trabert, Anthony "Tony"	United States	1970
Van Ryn, John	United States	1963
Sánchez Vicario, Arantxa	Spain	2007
Vilas, Guillermo	Argentina	1991
Vines, Henry Ellsworth	United States	1962
von Cramm, Gottfried	Germany	1977
Wallach, Maud Barger	United States	1958
Ward, Holcombe	United States	1956
Washburn, Watson	United States	1965
Whitman, Malcolm	United States	1955
Wightman, Hazel Hotchkiss	United States	1957
Wilander, Mats	Sweden	2002
Wilding, Anthony "Tony"	New Zealand	1978
Williams, Richard	United States	1957
Wood, Sidney	United States	1964
Wrenn, Robert "Bob"	United States	1955
Wright, Beals	United States	1956
Wade, Virginia	Great Britain	1989
Wagner, Marie	United States	1969
Woodbridge, Todd	Australia	2010

| Woodforde, Mark | Australia | 2010 |
| Zvereva, Natalya "Natasha" | Belarus | 2010 |

Nationalities

Country	# of members
United States	121
Australia	25
Great Britain	24
France	10
Sweden	5
Spain	4
Germany	
Czech Republic	
Argentina	2
Brazil	
Italy	
South Africa	
Romania	1
Ecuador	
Ireland	
Mexico	
New Zealand	
Norway	
Peru	
Yugoslavia	

See also

- Tenniseum

External links

- International Tennis Hall of Fame [7] Official Site
- 11 Intriguing Items at the International Tennis Hall of Fame [1] article
- International Tennis Hall of Fame [2] article

Geographical coordinates: 41°28′58″N 71°18′30″W

Overview of Providence

Providence, Rhode Island

City of Providence	
— City —	
Providence skyline seen looking north over the Providence River	
Seal	
Nickname(s): The Creative Capital, Beehive of Industry, The Renaissance City, The Divine City	
Location of Providence in Providence County, Rhode Island.	
Coordinates: 41°49′25″N 71°25′20″W	
Country	United States
State	Rhode Island
County	Providence
Government	
- Mayor	David Cicilline (D)
Area	
- City	20.5 sq mi (53.1 km^2)
- Land	18.5 sq mi (47.9 km^2)

- Water	2.1 sq mi (5.4 km^2)
Elevation	75 ft (23 m)
Population (2009)	
- City	171,909
- Density	9950/sq mi (3841.7/km^2)
- Metro	1630956
Time zone	EST (UTC-5)
- Summer (DST)	EDT (UTC-4)
Area code(s)	401
FIPS code	44-59000
GNIS feature ID	1219851
Airport	T.F. Green State Airport (Providence, RI) – PVD (Regional/State)
Website	http://www.providenceri.com

Providence is the capital and the most populous city of the U.S. state of Rhode Island, and one of the first cities established in the United States. Located in Providence County, it is the estimated second or third largest city[a][>] in the New England region. Despite the city proper only having an estimated population of 171,909 as of 2009, it anchors the 36th largest metropolitan population in the country, with an estimated MSA population of 1,600,856, exceeding that of Rhode Island by about 60% due to its reaching into southern Massachusetts. Situated at the mouth of the Providence River, at the head of Narragansett Bay, the city's small footprint is crisscrossed by seemingly erratic streets and contains a rapidly changing demographic.

Providence was founded in 1636 by Roger Williams, a religious exile from the Massachusetts Bay Colony. He named the area in honor of "God's merciful Providence" which he believed was responsible for revealing such a haven for him and his followers to settle. After being one of the first cities in the country to industrialize, Providence became noted for its jewelry and silverware industry. Today, the City of Providence is home to eight hospitals and seven institutions of higher learning, which has shifted the city's economy into service industries, though it still retains significant manufacturing activity.

Once nicknamed the "Beehive of Industry", Providence began rebranding itself as the "Creative Capital" in 2009 to emphasize its educational resources and arts community. Its previous moniker was "The Renaissance City", though its 2000 poverty rate was still among the ten highest for cities over 100,000.

History

Main article: History of Providence

Providence in the mid-nineteenth century

Routes of Washington and Rochambeau in 1781

NPS map of the W3R Route

The area which is now Providence was first settled in June 1636 by Roger Williams, and was one of the original Thirteen Colonies of the United States. Williams secured a title from the Narragansett natives around this time and gave the city its present name. Williams also cultivated Providence as a refuge for persecuted religious dissenters, as he himself had been exiled from Massachusetts. Providence's growth would be slow during the next quarter-century—the subsuming of its territory into surrounding towns, difficulty of farming the land, and differing of local traditions and land conflicts all slowed development.

In the mid-1770s, the British government levied taxes that impeded Providence's maritime, fishing and agricultural industries, the mainstay of the city's economy. One example was the Sugar Act, which was a tax levied against Providence's distilleries that adversely affected its trade in rum and slaves. These taxes caused Providence to join the other colonies in renouncing allegiance to the British Crown. In response to enforcement of unpopular trade laws, Providence residents spilled the first blood of the American Revolution in the notorious Gaspée Affair of 1772.

Though during the Revolutionary War the city escaped enemy occupation, the capture of nearby Newport disrupted industry and kept the population on alert. Troops were quartered for various campaigns and Brown University's University Hall was used as a barracks and military hospital.

After departing from Newport, French troops sent by King Louis XVI and commanded by the Comte de Rochambeau passed through Providence on their way to join the attack against British forces. The march from Newport to Providence was the beginning of a campaign led jointly by General George Washington in a decisive march that ended with the defeat of General Cornwallis in the Siege of Yorktown at Yorktown, Virginia and the Battle of the Chesapeake.

Following the war, Providence was the country's ninth-largest city.[b][>] with 7,614 people. The economy shifted from maritime endeavors to manufacturing, particularly machinery, tools, silverware, jewelry and textiles. By the turn of the twentieth century, Providence boasted some of the largest manufacturing plants in the country, including Brown & Sharpe, Nicholson File, and Gorham Silverware. The city's industries attracted many immigrants from Ireland, Germany, Sweden, England, Italy, Portugal, Cape Verde, and French Canada. Economic and demographic shifts caused social strife, notably with a series of race riots between whites and blacks during the 1820s. In response to these troubles and the economic growth, Providence residents ratified a city charter in 1831 as the population passed 17,000.

During the Civil War, local politics split over slavery as many had ties to Southern cotton. Despite ambivalence concerning the war, the number of military volunteers routinely exceeded quota, and the city's manufacturing proved invaluable to the Union. Postwar, horsecar lines covering the city enabled its growth and Providence thrived with waves of immigrants and land annexations bringing the population from 54,595 in 1865 to 175,597 by 1900.

The city's boom began to wane in the mid-1920s as industries, notably textiles, shut down. Jewelry manufacturing continued to grow, taking up the slack and employing many of the city's new immigrants, coming from Portuguese, Italian, Polish, Lithuanian and Jewish backgrounds. A number of hospitals also opened. The Great Depression hit the city hard, and Providence's downtown was subsequently flooded by the New England Hurricane of 1938. Though the city received a boost from World War II, this ended with the war. The city saw further decline as a result of nation-wide trends, with the construction of highways and increased suburbanization. The population would drop by 38% over the next three decades. From the 1950s to the 1980s, Providence was a notorious bastion of organized crime. The mafia boss Raymond L.S. Patriarca ruled a vast criminal enterprise.

The city's eponymous "Renaissance" began in the 1970s. From 1975 until 1982, $606 million of local and national Community Development funds were invested throughout the city, and the hitherto falling population began to stabilize. In the 1990s, Mayor Vincent Cianci, Jr showcased the city's strength in arts and pushed for further revitalization, ultimately resulting in the uncovering of the city's natural rivers (which had been paved over), relocation of a large section of railroad underground, creation of Waterplace Park and river walks along the river's banks, and construction of the Fleet Skating Rink (now the Bank of America Skating Rink) downtown and the 1.4 million ft² Providence Place Mall.

New investment triggered within the city, with new construction including numerous condo projects, hotels, and a new office high-rise all filling in the freed space. Despite new investment, poverty remains an entrenched problem as it does in most post-industrial New England cities. Nearly 30 percent of the city population lives below the poverty line. Recent increases in real estate values further exacerbate problems for those at marginal income levels, as Providence had the highest rise in median housing price of any city in the United States from 2004 to 2005.

Geography

The Providence city limits enclose a small geographic region, with a total area of 20.5 square miles (53.2 km²). 18.5 square miles (47.8 km²) of it is land and the remaining 2.1 square miles (5.3 km²) (roughly 10%) of it is water.

Providence is located at the head of Narragansett Bay, with the Providence River running into the bay through the center of the city, formed by the confluence of the Moshassuck and Woonasquatucket Rivers. The Waterplace Park amphitheater and riverwalks line the river's banks through downtown.

Providence is one of many cities claimed, like Rome, to be founded on seven hills. The more prominent hills are: Constitution Hill (near downtown), College Hill (east of the Providence River), and Federal Hill (west of downtown and is New England's largest Italian district outside of Massachusetts). The other four are: Tockwotten Hill at Fox Point, Smith Hill (where the State House is located), Christian Hill at Hoyle Square (junction of Cranston & Westminster Streets), and Weybosset Hill at the lower end of Weybosset Street, which was leveled in the early 1880s.

Neighborhoods

Main article: Neighborhoods in Providence

Providence has 25 official neighborhoods, though these neighborhoods are often grouped together and referred to collectively:

- The East Side is a region comprising the neighborhoods of Blackstone, Hope (aka Summit), Mount Hope, College Hill, Wayland, and Fox Point.

- The Jewelry District describes the area enclosed by I-95, I-195, and the Providence River.

- The North End is formed by the combination of the neighborhoods of Charles and Wanskuck.

- The South Side (or South Providence) consists of the neighborhoods of Elmwood, Lower South Providence, Upper South Providence, and the West End.

- West Broadway is an officially recognized neighborhood with its own association. It overlaps with the southern half of Federal Hill and the northern part of the West End.

- The West Side is a vague term sometimes used to mean the West End, Olneyville, Silver Lake, and nearby parts of abutting neighborhoods.

Cityscape

The city of Providence is geographically very compact, characteristic of eastern seaboard cities which developed prior to use of the automobile. It is among the most densely populated cities in the country. For this reason, Providence has the eighth-highest percentage of pedestrian commuters. The street layout is somewhat chaotic—over one thousand streets (a great number for the city's size) run haphazardly, connecting and radiating from traditionally bustling places like Market Square.

Downtown Providence has numerous 19th century mercantile buildings in the Federal and Victorian architectural styles, as well as several post-modern and modernist buildings, are located throughout this area. In particular, a fairly clear spatial separation appears between the areas of pre-1980s development and post-1980s development. West Exchange Street and Exchange Terrace serve as rough boundaries between the two.

The newer area, sometimes called "Capitol Center", includes Providence Place Mall (1999), a Westin hotel (1993) and The Residences at the Westin (2007), GTECH (2006), Waterplace condominiums (2007), and Waterplace Park (1994); the area tends toward newer development since much of it is land reclaimed in the 1970s from a mass of railroad tracks which was referred to colloquially as the "Chinese Wall". This part of Downtown is characterized by open spaces, wide roads, and intent landscaping.

The historic part of downtown has many streetscapes that look as they did eighty years ago. Many of the state's tallest buildings are found here. The largest structure, to date, is the art-deco-styled former Industrial Trust Tower, currently the Bank of America Building at 426 feet (130 m). By contrast, nearby to it is the second tallest One Financial Plaza, designed in modern taut-skin cladding, constructed a half century later. In between the two is 50 Kennedy Plaza. The Textron Tower is also a core building to the modest Providence skyline. Downtown is also the home of the Providence Biltmore and Westminster Arcade, the oldest enclosed shopping mall in the U.S., built in 1828.

The city's southern waterfront, away from the downtown core, is the location of many oil tanks, a docking station for a ferry boat, a non-profit sailing center, bars, strip clubs, and power plants. The Russian Submarine Museum was located here until 2008, after the submarine sank in a storm and was declared a loss. The Fox Point Hurricane Barrier is also found here, built to protect Providence from storm surge, like that it had endured in the 1938 New England Hurricane and again in 1954 from Hurricane Carol.

The majority of the cityscape comprises abandoned and revitalized industrial mills, double and triple decker housing (though the row houses found so commonly in other Northeast cities, are notably rare here), a small number of high-rise buildings (predominantly for housing the elderly), and single family homes. I-95 serves as a physical barrier between the city's commercial core and neighborhoods such as Federal Hill and the West End.

Climate

Providence's climate is between humid continental climate and humid subtropical climate, with warm summers, cold winters, and high humidity year-round. The USDA rates the city at Zone 6a, which is an "in-between" climate. The influence of the Atlantic Ocean keeps Providence, and the rest of the state of Rhode Island, warmer than many inland locales in New England. January is the coldest month with a mean of 28.7 °F (−1.8 °C). July is the warmest month with an average of 73.3 °F (22.9 °C), with highs rising to 90 °F (32 °C) on 10 days per summer. Extremes range from −17 °F (−27 °C) in February 1934 to 104 °F (40 °C) in August 1975.

As with the rest of the northeastern seaboard, Providence receives ample precipitation year-round. Monthly precipitation ranges from a high of 4.43 inches (112.5 mm) in March to a low of 3.17 inches (80.5 mm) in July. Precipitation levels are generally slightly lesser in the summer months than the winter months, when powerful storms known as Nor'easters can cause significant snowfall and blizzard conditions. Although hurricanes are not frequent in coastal New England, Providence's location at the head of Narragansett Bay makes it vulnerable to them.

Month	Jan	Feb	Mar	Apr	May	Jun	Jul	Aug	Sep	Oct	Nov	Dec	Year
Record high °F (°C)	69 (20.6)	72 (22.2)	90 (32.2)	98 (36.7)	95 (35)	98 (36.7)	102 (38.9)	104 (40)	100 (37.8)	88 (31.1)	81 (27.2)	77 (25)	104 (40)
Average high °F (°C)	37.1 (2.83)	39.3 (4.06)	47.7 (8.72)	58.1 (14.5)	68.5 (20.28)	77.3 (25.17)	82.6 (28.11)	80.9 (27.17)	73.4 (23)	62.9 (17.17)	52.4 (11.33)	42.1 (5.61)	60.2 (15.67)
Average low °F (°C)	20.3 (-6.5)	22.5 (-5.28)	30.0 (-1.11)	39.1 (3.94)	48.8 (9.33)	57.9 (14.39)	64.1 (17.83)	62.8 (17.11)	54.5 (12.5)	43.1 (6.17)	35.1 (1.72)	25.6 (-3.56)	42.0 (5.56)
Record low °F (°C)	−13	−17	1 (-17.2)	11 (-11.7)	29 (-1.7)	39 (3.9)	48 (8.9)	40 (4.4)	32 (0)	20 (-6.7)	6 (-14.4)	−12	−17
Precipitation inches (mm)	4.37 (111)	3.45 (87.6)	4.43 (112.5)	4.16 (105.7)	3.66 (93)	3.38 (85.9)	3.17 (80.5)	3.90 (99.1)	3.70 (94)	3.69 (93.7)	4.40 (111.8)	4.14 (105.2)	46.46 (1180.1)
Snowfall inches (cm)	10.6 (26.9)	9.0 (22.9)	4.9 (12.4)	0.7 (1.8)	0.3 (0.8)	0 (0)	0 (0)	0 (0)	0 (0)	0 (0)	1.4 (3.6)	6.0 (15.2)	32.9 (83.6)
Avg. precipitation days (≥ 0.01 in)	11.2	9.8	12.3	11.5	11.8	10.5	8.8	9.2	8.9	8.9	10.0	12.0	124.9
Avg. snowy days (≥ 0.1 in)	5.5	5.1	3.3	0.7	0.1	0	0	0	0	0	0.8	3.8	19.3
Sunshine hours	170.5	175.2	217.0	225.0	254.2	273.0	291.4	263.5	234.0	207.7	147.0	148.8	2607.3

Climate data for Providence, Rhode Island

Source #1: The Weather Channel (records)

Source #2: NOAA (1971-2000) , HKO (sun, 1961-1990)

Demographics

Historical populations		
Year	Pop.	%±
1790	6380	—
1800	7614	19.3%
1810	10070	32.3%
1820	11767	16.9%
1830	16833	43.1%
1840	23171	37.7%
1850	41513	79.2%
1860	50666	22.0%
1870	68904	36.0%
1880	104857	52.2%
1890	132146	26.0%
1900	175597	32.9%
1910	223326	27.2%
1920	237595	6.4%
1930	252981	6.5%
1940	253504	0.2%
1950	248674	−1.9%
1960	207498	−16.6%
1970	179213	−13.6%
1980	156804	−12.5%
1990	160728	2.5%
2000	173618	8.0%
2009	171909	−1.0%
Largest Cities and Other Urban Places in the United States: 1790 to 1990. Annual Estimates of the Population for Incorporated Places Over 100,000.		

As of the census of 2000, the population comprised 173,618 people, 162,389 households, and 35,859 families. The population density was 3,629.4/km² (9,401.7/sq mi), characteristic of comparatively older cities in New England such as New Haven, Connecticut; Boston, Massachusetts and Hartford,

Connecticut. Also like these cities, its population peaked in the 1940s just prior to the nationwide period of rapid suburbanization.

Providence has had a substantial Italian population since the turn of the century, with 14% (a plurality[b]) of the population claiming Italian ancestry. Italian influence manifests itself in Providence's Little Italy in Federal Hill. Irish immigrants have also had considerable influence on the city's history, with 8% of residents claiming Irish heritage.

Belying Providence's traditionally white makeup is the sizable minority presence it has acquired in the last twenty years. Though nearby cities like Boston and Hartford have longer-standing black and Latino communities, Providence now surpasses both in the density of its minority population, with non-Hispanic whites comprising less than half (40.9%) of the population. Though salient contributions to this growth have been among Asians and unspecified races, the most dramatic change comes from Hispanics, whose presence has increased fivefold. Having origins in Puerto Rico, Colombia, Bolivia, the Dominican Republic, and Central America (particularly Guatemala), Hispanics have strong influence in the neighborhoods of Elmwood, the West End, and Upper and Lower South Providence. Hispanic impact is even larger in the city's schools. Hispanics represent over half (55%) of all students in the city's school system while comprising only 36% of Providence's population.

In addition, Providence, like the nearby Massachusetts cities of Fall River and New Bedford, has a considerable community of immigrants from various Portuguese-speaking countries, living mostly in the areas of Washington Park and Fox Point. Portuguese is the city's third-largest nationality, (after Italian and Irish) at 4% of the population while Cape Verdeans make up another 2%.

African Americans constitute approximately 17% of the city with the largest percentages in Fox Point and Upper and Lower South Providence neighborhoods. Asians are 6% of Providence's population and have enclaves scattered throughout the city. Another 6% of the city has multiracial ancestry. Native Americans and Pacific Islanders make up the remaining 1.3%. With Liberians comprising .4% of the population, the city is home to the one of the three largest Liberian immigrant populations in the country.

The Providence metropolitan area, which includes Providence, Fall River, Massachusetts, and Warwick is estimated to be 1,622,520. In 2006, this area was officially added to the Boston Combined Statistical Area (CSA), the fifth-largest CSA in the country. In the last fifteen years, Providence has experienced a sizable growth in its under-18 population, attributed to the influx of Hispanics. The median age of the city is 28 years, while the largest age cohort is 20 to 24 year olds, owing to the city's large student population.

The per capita income, as of the 2000 census, was $15,525, which is well below both the state average of $29,113, and the national average of $21,587. The median income for a household was $26,867, and the median income for a family in Providence was $32,058, according to the 2000 census. The city has one of the highest rates of poverty in the nation with 29.1% of the population and 23.9% of families living below the poverty line in 2000, the largest concentrations being found in the city's Olneyville, and Upper and Lower South Providence areas. Poverty has affected children at a disproportionately higher rate with 40.1% of those under the age of 18 living below the poverty line, concentrated particularly west of downtown in the neighborhoods of Hartford, Federal Hill, and Olneyville.

Crime

Compared to the national average, Providence has a higher rate of property crime and an average rate of violent crime per 100,000 inhabitants. In 2009, there were 24 murders, the highest number since 2000 and a jump from the previous year's 13. Crime in all categories had been dropping substantially during 2002-2007, contrary to national trends. The nearby city of Worcester, Massachusetts which is about the same size had six murders in 2009 by comparison. The much larger city of Boston had 42. The police chief asserted that such violence was not stranger-to-stranger, but relationship driven. The pattern of violent crime was highly specific by neighborhood with vast majority of the murders taking place in the poorest sections of Providence, such as Washington Park, Fox Point Elmwood, South Providence and the West End.

In 2003, of the 239 United States cities with populations over 100,000, Providence's violent crime rate ranked 84th, as compared with New York City at 94th and Boston at 28th. Providence has the fifth-highest rate of property crime per 100,000 inhabitants in the country. Burglary and car theft, in particular constitute 1.12 and 2.49 times the national average.

Economy

Providence was one of the first cities to industrialize in the United States. By 1830, the city had manufacturing industries in metals, machinery, textiles, jewelry, and silverware. Though manufacturing has declined, the city is still one of the largest centers for jewelry and silverware design and manufacturing. Services, particularly education, health care, and finance, also make up a large portion of the city's economy. Providence also is the site of a sectional center facility, a regional hub for the U.S. Postal Service. Since it is the capital of Rhode Island, Providence's economy additionally consists of government services.

Largest Providence employers

Rank	Employer	Number of employees
1	Rhode Island Hospital[d][b]	6800
2	Brown University	5450
3	U.S. Postal Service	4500
4	Women & Infants Hospital of Rhode Island	3640

5	Miriam Hospital	2000
6	Bank of America	1725
7	Verizon	1400

The Fortune 500 conglomerate Textron and Fortune 1000 company Nortek Incorporated are both headquartered in the city, and GTECH's world headquarters has recently been moved to downtown Providence. Citizens Bank is also headquartered in Providence. Another company whose origins were in the city is Fleet Bank. Once Rhode Island's largest bank, it moved its headquarters to Boston, Massachusetts, after acquiring Shawmut Bank in 1995. Before its acquisition by Bank of America, Fleet merged with BankBoston to become New England's largest commercial bank.

The city is home to the Rhode Island Convention Center, which opened in December 1993. Along with a hotel, the convention center is connected to the Providence Place Mall, a major retail center, through a skywalk. The Port of Providence, the second largest deepwater seaport in New England, handles cargo such as cement, chemicals, heavy machinery, petroleum, and scrap metal.

Government

Providence serves as Rhode Island's capital, housing the Rhode Island General Assembly as well as the offices of the Governor and the Lieutenant Governor in the Rhode Island State House.

Providence's city government has a mayor-council form of government. The Providence City Council consists of fifteen city councilors, one for each of the city's wards. The council is tasked with enacting ordinances and passing an annual budget. Providence also has probate and superior courts. The U.S. District Court for the District of Rhode Island is located downtown across from City Hall adjacent to Kennedy Plaza.

David N. Cicilline was elected mayor by a large margin in 2002 and was re-elected without any major opposition in 2006. Cicilline is the first openly gay mayor of an American state capital. (notably, the second was elected 8 years later in neighboring Hartford, Connecticut.) Providence was the largest American city to have an openly gay mayor, until Sam Adams took office in Portland, Oregon on January 1, 2009.

Education

Postsecondary

Seven of the fourteen institutions of higher learning in Rhode Island have campuses in Providence (city proper):

Hope College and Manning Hall at Brown University

- Brown University, an Ivy League university
- Community College of Rhode Island (Downcity and Liston campuses)
- Johnson & Wales University, notable for its culinary and hospitality program
- Providence College, a Catholic college and member of the Big East Conference.

- Rhode Island College
- Roger Williams University
- Rhode Island School of Design (RISD), one of the country's top art colleges
- University of Rhode Island (Providence campus).

Between these schools the number of postsecondary students is approximately 44,000, or 25% the population of Providence. Compounded by Brown University's being the second-largest employer, higher education exerts a considerable presence in the city's politics and economy.

Private and charter schools

Several private schools, including Moses Brown, the Lincoln School, and the Wheeler School, are in the city's East Side. LaSalle Academy is located in the Elmhurst area of the city near Providence College. The public charter schools Time Squared Academy (K-12) and Textron Chamber of Commerce (9-12) are funded by GTECH and Textron respectively. In addition, the city's South Side houses Community Preparatory School, a private school serving primarily low-income students in grades 3-8. Within the semi-private schools, The Metropolitan Regional Career and Technical Center (The Met) and The Big Picture Company schools serve students through real world experiences and project-based learning. There are two separate centers for students with special needs.

Public schools

The Providence Public School District serves about 30,000 students from pre-Kindergarten to grade 12. The district has 25 elementary schools, nine middle schools, and thirteen high schools. The Providence Public School District features magnet schools at the middle and high school level, Nathanael Greene and Classical respectively. The overall graduation rate as of 2007 is 70.1%, which is close to the statewide rate of 71% and the national average of 70%.

Culture

See also: Media in Providence

Much of Providence culture is synonymous with Rhode Island culture. Like the state, the city has a non-rhotic accent which can be heard on local media. Providence also shares Rhode Island's affinity for coffee, as the former has the most coffee/doughnut shops per capita of any city in the country. Providence is also reputed to have the highest number of restaurants per capita, many of which are founded and/or staffed by its own Johnson & Wales graduates.

The Providence Performing Arts Center

The gateway arch over Atwells Avenue is a Federal Hill landmark. A sculpture of a pignoli cluster hangs from the center.

Providence has several ethnic neighborhoods, notably Federal Hill and the North End (Italian), Fox Point (Cape Verdean and Portuguese), West End (mainly Central American and Asians), and Smith Hill (Irish with miscellaneous enclaves of other groups). There are also many dedicated community organizations and arts associations located in the city.

The city gained the reputation as one of the most active and growing LGBT communities in the Northeast; the rate of reported gay and lesbian relationships is 75% higher than the national average and Providence has been named among the "Best Lesbian Places to Live". The current mayor, David Cicilline, won his election running as an openly gay man, making him the first openly gay mayor of a U.S. state capital. Former Mayor Cianci instituted the position of Mayor's Liaison to the Gay and Lesbian community in the 1990s. There are numerous social and community organizations supporting the gay, lesbian, bisexual, and transgender community. Providence is home to the largest gay bathhouse in New England.

During the summer months, the city regularly hosts WaterFire, an environmental art installation that consists of about 100 bonfires that blaze just above the surface of the three rivers that pass through the middle of downtown Providence. There are multiple Waterfire events that are accompanied by various pieces of classical and world music. The public art displays, most notably sculptures, change on a regular basis.

The city is also the home of the Tony Award-winning theater group Trinity Repertory Company, the Providence Black Repertory Company, and the Rhode Island Philharmonic Orchestra. Providence is also the home of several performing arts centers such as the Veterans Memorial Auditorium, the Providence Performing Arts Center, and the Providence Festival Ballet. The city's underground music scene, centered around artist-run spaces such as the now-defunct Fort Thunder, is known in underground music circles.

Sites of interest

See also: List of Registered Historic Places in Providence, Rhode Island

Providence is home to an 1200-acre (4.9 km^2) park system, notably Waterplace Park and Riverwalk, Roger Williams Park, Roger Williams National Memorial, and Prospect Terrace Park, the latter featuring expansive views of the downtown area. As one of the first cities in the country, Providence contains many historic buildings while the East Side neighborhood in particular includes the largest contiguous area of buildings listed on the National Register of Historic Places in the U.S. with many pre-revolutionary houses. The East Side is also home to the First Baptist Church

Old Stone Bank and Unitarian Church

in America, the oldest Baptist church in the Americas, founded by Roger Williams in 1638, as well as the Old State House, which served as the state's capitol from 1762 to 1904. Nearby is Roger Williams National Memorial. Downcity Providence is home to the fourth largest unsupported dome in the world (the second largest marble dome after St. Peter's Basilica in Rome), as well as the Westminster Arcade, which is the oldest enclosed shopping center in the U.S.

Providence Catholic Cathedral and environs

The main art museum is the Rhode Island School of Design Museum, which has the twentieth largest collection in the country. The city's southern waterfront hosts a decommissioned Cold War era Russian submarine. In addition to the Providence Public Library and its nine branches, the city is home to the Providence Athenæum, the fourth oldest library in the country. Here, on one of his many visits to Providence, Edgar Allan Poe, met and courted a love interest named Sarah Helen Whitman. Poe was a regular fixture there, as was H. P. Lovecraft; both of them influential writers of gothic literature.

The Bank of America Skating Center, formerly the Fleet Skating Center, is located near Kennedy Plaza in the downtown district, connected by pedestrian tunnel to Waterplace Park, a cobblestone and concrete park below street traffic that abuts Providence's three rivers.

The southern part of the city is home to the famous roadside attraction Nibbles Woodaway (also known as the "Big Blue Bug"), the world's largest termite, as well as the aforementioned Roger Williams Park, which contains a zoo, a botanical center, and the Museum of Natural History and Planetarium.

Sports

The city is home to the American Hockey League team Providence Bruins, which plays at the Dunkin' Donuts Center (formerly the Providence Civic Center). From 1926 to 1972, the AHL's Providence Reds (renamed the Rhode Island Reds in their last years) played at the Rhode Island Auditorium. In 1972, the team relocated to the Providence Civic Center, where they played until moving to Binghamton, New York, in 1977.

Providence has its own roller derby league. Formed in 2004, it currently has four teams: the Providence Mob Squad, the Sakonnet River Roller Rats, the Old Money Honeys, and the Rhode Island Riveters. The NFL's New England Patriots and MLS's New England Revolution play in Foxborough, Massachusetts, which is situated halfway between Providence and Boston. Providence was formerly home to two major league franchises: the NFL's Providence Steam Roller in the 1920s and 1930s, and the NBA's Providence Steamrollers in the 1940s. The city is also where Rocky Marciano won 29 of his 49 fights.

The city's defunct baseball team, the Providence Grays, competed in the National League from 1879 through 1885. The team defeated the New York Metropolitans in baseball's first successful "world championship series" in 1884. In 1914, after the Boston Red Sox purchased Babe Ruth from the then-minor league Baltimore Orioles, the team prepared Ruth for the major leagues by sending him to finish the season playing for a minor league team in Providence that was also known as the Grays. Today, professional baseball is offered by the Pawtucket Red Sox, the AAA affiliate of the Boston Red Sox which plays in nearby Pawtucket. Most baseball fans—along with the local media—tend to follow the Boston Red Sox.

Major colleges and universities fielding NCAA Division I athletic teams are Brown University and Providence College. The latter is a member of the Big East Conference. Much local hype is associated with games between these two schools or the University of Rhode Island. Providence has also hosted the alternative sports event Gravity Games from 1999 to 2001, and was also the first host of ESPN's X Games, known in its first edition as the Extreme Games, in 1995.

Infrastructure

Health and medicine

Providence is home to eight hospitals, most prominently Rhode Island Hospital, the largest general acute care hospital in the state. The hospital is in a complex along I-95 that includes Hasbro Children's Hospital and Women and Infants Hospital. The city is also home to the Roger Williams Medical Center, St. Joseph Hospital For Specialty Care (a division of St. Joseph Health Services Of Rhode Island), The Miriam Hospital, a major teaching affiliate associated with the Alpert Medical School of Brown University, as well as a VA medical center.

Providence is home to the Quality Assurance Review Center (QARC), which performs thousands of radiotherapy reviews per year. QARC is primarily supported by grants from the National Cancer Institute (NCI) and contracts from the pharmaceutical industry. It receives radiotherapy data from around one-thousand hospitals in both the United States and abroad. The center also maintains a strategic affiliation with the University of Massachusetts Medical School in Worcester, Massachusetts.

The Rhode Island Blood Center has its main headquarters in Providence. Since 1979, the Rhode Island Blood Center has been the sole organization in charge of blood collection and testing and distribution of blood products to 11 hospitals in Rhode Island.

Transportation

Providence is served by air primarily by the commercial airfield T. F. Green Airport in nearby Warwick. General aviation fields also serve the region. Due to overcrowding and Big Dig complications in Boston, Massport has been promoting T.F. Green as an alternative to Boston's Logan International Airport.

Providence Station

Providence Station, located between the Rhode Island State House and the downtown district, is served by Amtrak and MBTA Commuter Rail services, with a commuter rail running to Boston. Approximately 2400 passengers daily pass through the station. Additionally, funds have been allocated to extend the commuter rail from Providence to T. F. Green Airport terminating at a $222.5 million intermodal station to be completed in 2009.

I-95 runs from north to south through Providence while I-195 connects the city to eastern Rhode Island and southeastern Massachusetts, including New Bedford, Massachusetts, and Cape Cod. I-295 encircles Providence while RI 146 provides a direct connection with Worcester, Massachusetts. The city has commissioned and begun a long-term project, the Iway, to move I-195 not only for safety reasons, but also to free up land and to reunify the Jewelry District with Downcity Providence, which had been split from one another by the highway. The project is estimated to cost $446 million and be completed in 2012.

RIPTA buses in front of Providence City Hall

Kennedy Plaza, in downtown Providence, serves as a transportation hub for local public transit as well as a departure point for Peter Pan. On a daily basis, there are over 75,000 public transportation citizens. and Greyhound bus lines. Public transit is managed by Rhode Island Public Transit Authority (RIPTA). Through RIPTA alone Kennedy Plaza serves over 71,000 people a day. The majority of the area covered by RIPTA is served by traditional buses. Of particular note is the East Side Trolley Tunnel running under College Hill, the use of which is reserved for RIPTA buses. RIPTA also operates the *Providence LINK*, a system of tourist trolleys in downtown Providence. From 2000 to 2008, RIPTA operated a seasonal ferry to Newport between May and October.

Utilities

Electricity and natural gas are provided by Narragansett Electric Company which is owned by National Grid USA. Providence Water is responsible for the distribution of drinking water, ninety percent of which comes from the Scituate Reservoir about ten miles (16 km) west of downtown, with contributions coming from four smaller bodies of water. Drinking water in Providence has consistently been rated among the highest quality in the US.

Sister cities

Providence has four sister cities designated by Sister Cities International:

- Phnom Penh, Cambodia
- Florence, Italy
- Riga, Latvia
- Santo Domingo, Dominican Republic

See also

- Notable people from Providence
- List of tallest buildings in Providence
- Neighborhoods in Providence

Notes

^ **a:** The US Census estimates Worcester, Massachusetts to have overtaken Providence in 2006 by 199 people. Though this is well within the margin of error, this article, Worcester, Massachusetts, and List of United States cities by population uses the 2006 estimates for purposes of ranking. The New England article, however, ranks by 2000 Census, which places Providence as second largest.

^ **b:** Providence was listed as a town (not a city) by the US Census Bureau until the Census of 1840. This is because in all the New England states, city status is conferred by the form of government, not population. Providence retained the title of ninth-largest settlement until the Census of 1810.

^ **c:** "Other" is the largest nationality group. Italian is the largest nationality by descendancy for a specified country.

^ **d:** Figure includes Hasbro Children's Hospital as part of Rhode Island Hospital.

Further reading

- "EDC Profile City of Providence" [1]. Rhode Island Economic Development Corporation. 2006.
- Samantha Cook, Greg Ward, Tim Perry (2004). "Providence". *The Rough Guide USA*. Rough Guides. pp. 243–247. ISBN 1-84353-262-X.
- Rich, Wilbur C. (2000). "Vincent Cianci and Boosterism in Providence, Rhode Island". *Governing Middle-Sized Cities*. Lynne Rienner Publishers. pp. 197–216. ISBN 1-55587-870-9.

External links

- The City of Providence website [2]
- Providence Warwick Convention & Visitors Bureau [3]
- Providence travel guide from Wikitravel
- Portrait of Providence from Altitude, 2010 [4], aerial photos by Doc Searles

1. REDIRECT Template:Navboxes

pnb:سنⵏیوورپ

Providence River

The **Providence River** is a tidal river in the U.S. state of Rhode Island. It flows approximately 8 miles (13 km). There are no dams along the river's length, although the Fox Point Hurricane Barrier is located south of downtown, to protect the city of Providence from damaging tidal floods.

Providence River looking south

The southern part of the river has been dredged at a cost of $65 million in federal and state funds to benefit nearby marinas and commercial shipping interests.

Course

The river is formed by the confluence of the Woonasquatucket and Moshassuck rivers in downtown Providence. One half mile downstream, it is joined from the east by the Seekonk River and continues south. The cities of Providence, Cranston, and Warwick lie to the west of the river, while the city of East Providence and the town of Barrington lie to the east. At the narrows between Conimicut Point, in Warwick to the west and Nayatt Point in Barrington

Point Street Bridge, spanning the Providence River

to the east, the Conimicut Shoal Lighthouse (http://www.lighthouse.cc/conimicut/) marks the entrance to the river from Narragansett Bay.

Crossings

Below is a list of all crossings over the Providence River. The list starts at the headwaters and goes downstream.

- Providence
  - Washington Place
  - College Street
  - Crawford Street
  - Interstate 195
  - Point Street
  - Fox Point Hurricane Barrier
  - Providence River Bridge (relocated Interstate 195)

Tributaries

- Seekonk River
- Pawtuxet River
- Moshassuck River
- Woonasquatucket River

See also

- Providence, Rhode Island
- List of rivers in Rhode Island
- Moshassuck River
- Pawtuxet River
- Seekonk River
- Warren River
- Woonasquatucket River
- Narragansett Bay

References

- Maps from the United States Geological Survey
- Providence.edu [1] Providence River Dredging Project Answer Sheet
- crmc.state.ri.us [2] Providence River Dredging Project: Breaking the Impasse through Partnering

Providence County, Rhode Island

Providence County, Rhode Island	
Location in the state of Rhode Island	
Rhode Island's location in the U.S.	
Founded	1703
Seat	Providence (1703-1842)
Largest city	Providence
Area **- Total** **- Land** **- Water**	436 sq mi (1129 km²) 413 sq mi (1070 km²) 23 sq mi (60 km²), 5.18%
Population[Est.] **- (2008)** **- Density**	626150 1505/sq mi (581/km²)
Congressional districts	1st, 2nd

Providence County is a county located in the U.S. state of Rhode Island. As of 2000, the population was 621,602. The center of population of Rhode Island is located in Providence County, in the city of Cranston [1]. It is the 97th most populous county in the United States.

History

Providence County was constituted on June 22, 1703, as the County of Providence Plantations. It consisted of five towns, namely Providence, Warwick, Westerly, Kingstown, and Greenwich and encompassed territory in present-day Kent and Washington counties. Washington County was split off in 1729, while Kent County was split off in 1750. The town of Cumberland was acquired from Massachusetts and added to Providence County in 1746-47, and the towns of East Providence and Pawtucket were made part of Providence County when the final border with Massachusetts was settled in 1862. County government in Rhode Island was abolished in 1842.

Geography

According to the U.S. Census Bureau, the county has a total area of 436 square miles (1,129 km²), of which 413 square miles (1,070 km²) is land and 23 square miles (58 km²) (5.18%) is water.

The highest point in the county is Jerimoth Hill, also the highest in the state. Sea level is the lowest point.

Adjacent Counties

- Norfolk County, Massachusetts - northeast
- Bristol County, Massachusetts - east
- Bristol County, Rhode Island - southeast
- Kent County, Rhode Island - south
- Windham County, Connecticut - west
- Worcester County, Massachusetts - northwest

National protected area

- Roger Williams National Memorial

Demographics

Historical populations		
Census	Pop.	%±
1790	24391	—
1800	25854	6.0%
1810	30769	19.0%
1820	35736	16.1%
1830	47018	31.6%
1840	58073	23.5%
1850	87526	50.7%
1860	107799	23.2%
1870	149190	38.4%
1880	197874	32.6%
1890	255123	28.9%
1900	328683	28.8%
1910	424353	29.1%
1920	475190	12.0%
1930	540016	13.6%
1940	550298	1.9%
1950	574973	4.5%
1960	568778	−1.1%
1970	580261	2.0%
1980	571349	−1.5%
1990	596270	4.4%
2000	621602	4.2%
Est. 2008	626150	0.7%

As of the census of 2000, there were 621,602 people, 239,936 households, and 152,839 families residing in the county. The population density was 1,504 people per square mile (581/km²). There were 253,214 housing units at an average density of 613 per square mile (237/km²). The racial makeup of the county was 78.38% White, 6.55% Black or African American, 0.51% Native American, 2.90% Asian, 0.07% Pacific Islander, 8.02% from other races, and 3.58% from two or more races. 13.39% of the population were Hispanic or Latino of any race. 19.0% were of Italian, 10.9% Irish, 8.1% French, 7.7%

Portuguese, 7.2% French Canadian and 5.8% English ancestry according to Census 2000. 72.7% spoke English, 13.4% Spanish, 4.9% Portuguese, 2.5% French and 1.6% Italian as their first language.

There were 239,936 households out of which 30.70% had children under the age of 18 living with them, 44.50% were married couples living together, 14.90% had a female householder with no husband present, and 36.30% were non-families. 29.80% of all households were made up of individuals and 11.90% had someone living alone who was 65 years of age or older. The average household size was 2.48 and the average family size was 3.11.

In the county, the population was spread out with 24.00% under the age of 18, 11.10% from 18 to 24, 29.80% from 25 to 44, 20.50% from 45 to 64, and 14.60% who were 65 years of age or older. The median age was 35 years. For every 100 females there were 91.80 males. For every 100 females age 18 and over, there were 87.90 males.

The median income for a household in the county was $36,950, and the median income for a family was $46,694. Males had a median income of $35,336 versus $26,322 for females. The per capita income for the county was $19,255. About 11.90% of families and 15.50% of the population were below the poverty line, including 22.30% of those under age 18 and 12.70% of those age 65 or over.

Providence County is 71% Catholic, making it among the most Catholic counties in the country.

Cities, towns, and villages

Villages are census division, but have no separate corporate existence from the towns they are in.

- Burrillville
  - *Harrisville (a village of Burrillville)*
  - *Pascoag (a village of Burrillville)*
- Central Falls
- Cranston
- Cumberland
  - *Cumberland Hill (a village of Cumberland)*
  - *Valley Falls (a village split between Cumberland and Lincoln)*
- East Providence
- Foster
- Glocester
- Johnston

- Lincoln

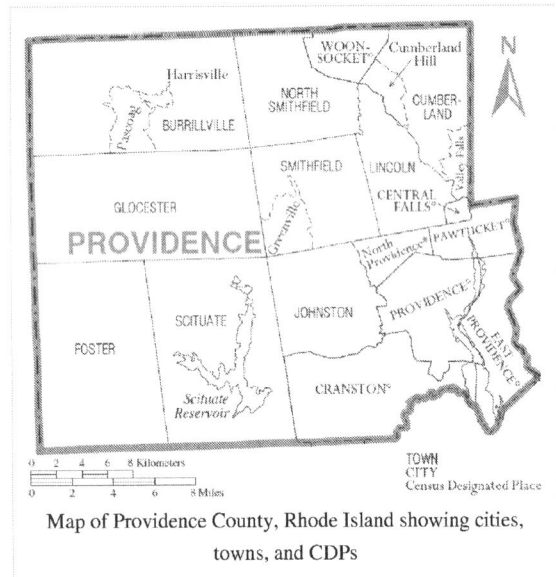

Map of Providence County, Rhode Island showing cities, towns, and CDPs

- *Manville (a village of Lincoln)*
- *Albion (a village of Lincoln)*
- *Quinnville (a village of Lincoln)*
- *Lonsdale (a village of Lincoln)*
- *Saylesville (a village of Lincoln)*
- *Lime Rock (a village of Lincoln)*
- North Providence
- North Smithfield

  - *Branch Village (a village of North Smithfield)*
  - *Forestdale (a village of North Smithfield)*
  - *Primrose (a village of North Smithfield)*
  - *Slatersville (a village of North Smithfield)*
  - *Union Village (a village of North Smithfield)*
  - *Waterford (a village of North Smithfield)*
- Pawtucket
- Providence
- Scituate
- Smithfield

  - *Greenville (a village of Smithfield)*
- Woonsocket

Trivia

The fictional town of Quahog, Rhode Island from the show *Family Guy* is located in Providence County.

See also

- List of Registered Historic Places in Providence County, Rhode Island

External links

- National Register of Historic Places listing for Providence Co., Rhode Island [2]

Geographical coordinates: 41°52′N 71°35′W

History of Providence

The Rhode Island city of Providence has a nearly four hundred-year history integral to that of the USA, including the first bloodshed of the American Revolution, economic shifts from trading to manufacturing, the decline of which contemporaneous to the Great Depression devastated the city, and eventual economic recovery through investment of public funds.

Providence, harbor view, 1858

Founding and colonial era

The area which is now Providence was first settled in June 1636 by Roger Williams, and was one of the original Thirteen Colonies of the United States. Williams had been exiled from the Massachusetts Bay Colony for his outspoken beliefs concerning distinction of state government and religion:

> All civil states, with their officers of justice, in their respective constitutions and administrations, are proved essentially civil and therefore not judges, governors, or defenders of the spiritual, or Christian, state and worship

— Roger Williams

Williams secured a title from the Narragansett natives around this time and gave the city its present name. Williams also cultivated Providence Plantations as a refuge for persecuted religious dissenters, as he himself had been exiled from Massachusetts. Providence Plantations was an agricultural and fishing community, though its lands were difficult to farm, and its borders were disputed with Connecticut and Massachusetts. During King Philip's War between the Wampanoag leader Metacomet (King Philip) and the English Colonists, the town of Providence was destroyed by a Native American coalition on March 29, 1676.

After the town was rebuilt, the economy expanded into more industrial and commercial activity. The outer lands of Providence Plantations, extending to the Massachusetts and Connecticut borders, were incorporated as Scituate, Glocester, and Smithfield in 1731. Later, Cranston, Johnston, and North Providence would also be carved out of Providence's municipal territory. By the 1760s, the population of the remaining urban core reached 4,000.

Revolutionary times to manufacturing

Providence's First Baptist Church in America was organized in 1636 and the present building occupied in 1776

In the mid-1770s, the British government levied taxes that impeded Providence's maritime, fishing and agricultural industries, the mainstay of the city's economy. One example was the Sugar Act, which impacted Providence's distilleries and its trade in rum and slaves. These taxes caused Providence to join the other colonies in renouncing allegiance to the British Crown.In response to enforcement of unpopular trade laws, Providence residents spilled the first blood of the American Revolution in the notorious Gaspée Affair of 1772.

Though during the Revolutionary War the city escaped enemy occupation, the capture of nearby Newport disrupted industry and kept the population on alert. Troops were quartered for various campaigns and Brown University's University Hall was used as a barracks and military hospital.

Following the war, the economy shifted from maritime endeavors to manufacturing, particularly machinery, tools, silverware, jewelry and textiles. At one time, Providence boasted some of the largest manufacturing plants in the country, including Brown & Sharpe, Nicholson File, and

A historic mill on the Woonasquatucket River

Gorham Silverware. The city's industries attracted many immigrants from Ireland, Germany, Sweden, England, Italy, Portugal, Cape Verde, and French Canada. Economic and demographic shifts caused social strife.Hard Scrabble and Snow Town were two African American neighborhoods that were the sites of two race riots in which working-class whites destroyed multiple black homes in 1824 and 1831, respectively. In response to these troubles and the economic growth, Providence residents ratified a city charter in 1831.

During the Civil War, local politics split over slavery as many had ties to Southern cotton. Despite ambivalence concerning the war, the number of military volunteers routinely exceeded quota, and the city's manufacturing proved invaluable to the Union.

Postwar, horsecar lines covering the city enabled its growth and Providence thrived with waves of immigrants and land annexations bringing the population from 54,595 in 1865 to 175,597 by 1900.

Decline

The city began to see a decline by the mid-1920s as industries, notably textiles, shut down. The Great Depression hit the city hard, and Providence's downtown was flooded by the New England Hurricane of 1938 soon after. The city saw further decline as a result of the nation-wide trends, with the construction of highways and increased suburbanization. From the 1950s to the 1980s, Providence was a notorious bastion of organized crime. The legendary mafia boss Raymond Patriarca ruled a vast criminal enterprise from the city for over three decades, during which murders and kidnapings would become commonplace.

"Renaissance"

The city's eponymous "Renaissance" began in the 1970s. From 1975 until 1982, $606 million of local and national Community Development funds from were invested throughout the city, and the hitherto falling population began to stabilize. In the 1990s, Mayor Vincent Cianci, Jr showcased the city's strength in arts and pushed for further revitalization, ultimately resulting in the opening up of the city's natural rivers (which had been paved over), relocation of a large section of railroad underground, creation of Waterplace Park and river walks along the river's banks, and construction of the Fleet Skating Rink (now the Bank of America Skating Rink) in downtown and the 1.4 million ft^2 Providence Place Mall.

New investment triggered within the city, with new construction including numerous condo projects, hotels, and a new office highrise all filling in the freed space. Despite new investment, poverty remains an entrenched problem as it does in most post-industrial New England cities. Nearly 30 percent of the city population lives below the poverty line. Recent increases in real estate values further exacerbate problems for those at marginal income levels, as Providence had the highest rise in median housing price of any city in the United States from 2004 to 2005.

Due to the recent inundation of proposals in Providence, the city has begun a planning process to decide how to holistically incorporate all projects in a way that preserves the fabric of the city, promotes future development, and capitalizes on the historic nature of the city and waterfront land Emphasis has been stressed on the following:

- Development of a new streetcar system
- Redevelopment of centrally located land freed up by the relocation of Interstate 195

- Riverfront improvements on the Woonasquatucket River west of Providence Place, creating continuous pedestrian access to the waterfront
- Redevelopment of the corridor south of Downcity between the Providence River and Interstate 95.

Notes

4. *Three and One-Half Centuries at a Glance* [1] ProvidenceRI.com - History and Fact.

References

- Lepore, Jill. (1998). *The Name of War: King Philip's War and the Origins of American Identity.* New York: Vintage Books. ISBN 0-375-70262-8.

Things to Do and See

Roger Williams National Memorial

Roger Williams National Memorial	
U.S. National Register of Historic Places	
Location:	Providence, Rhode Island
Coordinates:	41°49′49″N 71°24′39″W
Built/Founded:	1636
Architect:	Norman Isham
Architectural style(s):	No Style Listed
Governing body:	Local
Added to NRHP:	October 15, 1966
NRHP Reference#:	66000942

Roger Williams National Memorial is a landscaped urban park located on a common lot of the original settlement of Providence, Rhode Island, by Roger Williams in 1636. Bounded by North Main,

Canal, and Smith Streets and Park Row, the memorial commemorates the life of the co-founder of the Colony of Rhode Island and Providence Plantations and a champion of the ideal of religious freedom. Williams, banished from Massachusetts for his beliefs, founded this colony as a refuge where all could come to worship as their conscience dictated without interference from the state. This park is the 20th smallest national park in the nation.

The park's visitor center features an exhibit and video about Roger Williams and the founding of Rhode Island, as well as information about historic sites in Providence.

View of Roger Williams National Memorial

Administrative history

The national memorial was authorized on October 22, 1965. As with all historic areas administered by the National Park Service, the memorial was listed on the National Register of Historic Places on October 15, 1966. As of 2006, it is the only unit of the National Park System in Rhode Island. Touro Synagogue National Historic Site in Newport is an affiliated area of the National Park Service, but not formally part of the system.

References

- *The National Parks: Index 2001–2003*. Washington: U.S. Department of the Interior.

External links

- Official NPS website: Roger Williams National Memorial [1]

Parks in Providence, Rhode Island
Burnside Park · India Point Park · Prospect Terrace Park · Roger Williams National Memorial · Roger Williams Park · Waterplace Park

Veterans Memorial Auditorium (Providence)

Veterans Memorial Auditorium--Masonic Temple	
U.S. National Register of Historic Places	
Location:	Providence, Rhode Island
Coordinates:	41°49′47.45″N 71°25′2.73″W
Built/Founded:	1927
Architect:	Multiple
Architectural style(s):	Classical Revival
Governing body:	Private
Added to NRHP:	November 16, 1993
NRHP Reference#:	93001181

Veterans Memorial Auditorium (VMA) is a performing arts theater in Providence, Rhode Island. Construction began in 1928, but was delayed by the Great Depression. The theater was finally completed in 1950. It is among the oldest arts venues in Rhode Island and is on the National Register of Historic Places. It was completely restored in 1990. The ornately-designed 1,931 seat concert hall houses the largest theater stage in Rhode Island and is considered to have some of the best acoustics in New England. The performance space features a gilded proscenium arch, allegorical and heraldic ceiling murals. The Rhode Island Philharmonic Orchestra holds several concerts at the VMA each year. In addition, the VMA hosts a broad range of events each season, offering a variety of performances, rehearsals, exhibitions, concerts, educational events, meetings, and other special events. Since 1950, when the theater opened, it had begun to fall into disrepair and in the early 1980s the state of Rhode Island was thinking of closing the auditorium and the adjoining Masonic Temple and reducing the complex to a parking lot. In 1983 the Veterans Memorial Auditorium Preservation Association (VMAPA) was formed to try and save the auditorium. They rallied for 5 years and in 1988 Governor

DiPrete awarded the VMAPA with $5 million for the VMA's renovation. Since that time it has been a center for the arts. The Renaissance Providence Hotel, formerly the Masonic Temple, is located directly adjacent to the VMA.

See also

- National Register of Historic Places listings in Providence, Rhode Island

Rhode Island School of Design Museum

<table>
<tr><td colspan="2" align="center">**Rhode Island School of Design Museum**</td></tr>
<tr><td colspan="2" align="center"></td></tr>
<tr><td>**Established**</td><td>1877</td></tr>
<tr><td>**Location**</td><td>224 Benefit Street
Providence, RI 02903-2723 United States</td></tr>
<tr><td>**Type**</td><td>Art</td></tr>
<tr><td>**Website**</td><td>Rhode Island School of Design Museum [1]</td></tr>
</table>

Rhode Island School of Design Museum is a prominent art museum in Providence, Rhode Island affiliated with the well-known Rhode Island School of Design. The museum was founded in 1877 and is the 20th largest art museum in the United States.

Collections

The Museum of Art, Rhode Island School of Design (The RISD Museum) contains a broad range of works from around the world, including Egypt, Asia, Africa, ancient Greece and Rome, Europe, and the Americas. It also features many notable works by a range Rhode Island artists such as 17th century Newport furniture makers Goddard and Townsend and nineteenth century Rhode Island painters, such as Anglo-American impressionist John Noble Barlow and portraitist Gilbert Stuart. The museum also features prominent international and American artists such as Picasso, Monet, Manet, Paul Revere, and Andy Warhol. The RISD Museum houses over 80,000 works of art.

Ancient Art

The department of Ancient Art includes bronze figural sculpture and vessels, an exceptional collection of Greek coins (that grew out of the collection donated by Henry A. Greene), stone sculpture, Greek vases, paintings, and mosaics, a fine collection of Roman jewelry and glass, and teaching examples of terracottas. A number of objects represent the most outstanding examples in their categories. Among these virtually unique works of art are an Etruscan bronze situla (pail), a fifth-century B.C. Greek female head in marble, and a rare Hellenistic bronze Aphrodite. Among the Greek vases are works by some of the major Attic painters, including Nikosthenes and the Providence, Brygos, Pan, Lewis, and Reed Painters. The cornerstone of the Museum's Egyptian collection is the Ptolemaic period coffin and mummy of the priest Nesmin. Among other highlights of the Egyptian collection are a rare New Kingdom ceramic paint box, a relief fragment from the Temple at Karnak, and a first-class collection of faience.

Asian Art

The department of Asian Art contains ceramics, costume, prints, painting, sculpture, and textiles. One of the highlights of the collection is the peerless group of over six hundred nineteenth-century Japanese bird-and-flower prints that were collected by Abby Aldrich Rockefeller. The collection of over 100 surimono (privately published woodblock prints) are considered the finest assemblage outside Japan. The Japanese prints are shown, in rotation, in galleries dedicated to their exhibition. A major attraction is the important 12th-century wooden Buddha Dainich Nyorai, the largest (over nine feet tall) historic Japanese wooden sculpture in the United States. The Buddha is on permanent exhibition in its own gallery.

The Japanese textiles are the core and glory of the Asian textile collection. The kesa, or Buddhist priests' robes, are the most numerous, with 104 examples. The 47 Japanese Noh robes, meticulously documented, form a comprehensive collection of nearly every type of costume in use in the Noh drama of eighteenth- and nineteenth-century Japan. Their spectacular colors and patterns, embellished with gold and silver, express perfectly the splendor of the traditional and highly stylized Noh theater. The Museum's collection of Indian saris and Chinese ceremonial robes is superb. Examples from these collections are shown in rotation with the Japanese textiles in the Lucy Truman Aldrich Gallery, which is devoted to the display of Asian textiles. The Islamic and Indian collections include works of art in all media that celebrate the artistic heritage of the Arab, Indian, Persian, and Turkish cultures.

Contemporary Art

Created in 2000, the department of Contemporary Art oversees an eclectic collection of painting, sculpture, video, mixed media, and interdisciplinary work, dating from 1960 to the present. In addition, the department regularly organizes exhibitions that highlight important issues, trends and individual explorations in recent art. Represented in the collection are significant paintings by Richard Anuskiewicz, Roy Lichtenstein, Robert Mangold, Agnes Martin, Sam Francis, Cy Twombly, Wayne Thiebaud, Larry Rivers, and Andy Warhol, among others. The collection also includes important sculptural work by Richard Artschwager, Louise Bourgeois, Louise Nevelson, Tom Otterness, Lucas Samaras, and Robert WilsonWikipedia:WikiProject Disambiguation/Fixing links. The museum's video collection features experimental works by such pioneers in the field as Vito Acconci, Lynda Benglis, Bruce Nauman, Martha Rosler, Richard Serra, and William Wegman.

The Nancy Sayles Day Collection of Latin American Art includes contemporary paintings by such important artists as Luís Cruz Azaceta, Fernando Botero, José Bedia, Claudio Bravo, Wifredo Lam,

Jesús Rafael Soto, Joaquín Torres Garcia, and Roberto Matta Echuarren.

The department has a natural and strong connection with Providenceís contemporary art community, and numerous RISD faculty and alumni and local artists are represented in the collection. Among them are Howard Ben Tré, Jonathan Bonner, Richard Fleischner, Ruth Dealy, Richard Merkin and[Bunny Harvey.

Costume and Textiles

The Museum has been actively exhibiting textiles for one hundred years and today the department of Costume and Textiles consists of over 15,000 objects, dating from antiquity to the present. The collection is divided roughly into eleven thousand flat textiles and four thousand costume and accessories that trace the history of fabric and dress. A collection of national significance, it contains outstanding examples of European and American costume and textiles from the 17th through 20th centuries, and is very strong in the areas of Peruvian, Coptic, African, Native American, Oceanic, and Asian textiles.

The Asian textiles are particularly rich. Those given by Lucy Truman Aldrich in the 1930s are among the best in this country. The Japanese Noh robes are generally considered the finest assemblage in the world. In addition, the collection of 19th-century Chinese robes displays the splendor of decoration, as well as the importance of social rank and status, in costume of the period. One of the earliest European textiles in the collection is an extremely rare medieval German embroidery fragment. Exquisite Italian and Spanish silks and velvets represent the height of luxury textiles in the 14th and 15th centuries. The department also cares for a large collection of European tapestries, the earliest of which dates from around 1520. Highlights of the European collection include an exquisite example of Elizabethan embroidery in the form of a man's nightcap, fine examples of 18th-century French and English costume, and an opulent train worn in the court of Napoleon. Examples from Charles Frederick Worth, Fortuny, Paul Poiret, and Liberty & Co.. represent European fashion design achievements of the 19th and early 20th centuries.

Included in the department are significant examples of early American needlework: quilts, coverlets, samplers, and embroideries. The collection also presents a remarkable survey of the development of printed textiles, an integral part of Rhode Island history. The Museum has a collection of New England needlework of great rarity, and a collection beyond compare of schoolgirl samplers made at the Balch School in Providence. Experimental work in textile design in the collection includes work by Diane Itter, Cynthia Schira, Jack Lenor Larson, and Junichi Arai. Among the important 20th-century designers represented in the collection are Charles James, Claire McCardell, Bonnie Cashin, Chanel, Halston and Geoffrey Beene. The department also houses more than three hundred early twentieth-century textiles and garments and eighteen cubic feet of records from Providence's Tirocchi Dressmakers' Shop (fl. 1915-1947). Such complete documentation of an historical dressmaking business exists nowhere else in the United States. Thus, in addition to the splendor of the objects themselves, the Tirocchi collection is an unparalleled resource for understanding many wide-ranging historical issues, including Italian immigration, women as workers and consumers, and the transition from hand production of garments to ready-to-wear clothing.

Decorative Arts

The Decorative Arts collection encompasses European and American decorative arts (furniture, silver and other metalwork, wallpaper, ceramics, and glass) from the Medieval period to the present. A major highlight of the department is the Charles L. Pendleton Collection of furniture made by 18th-century Boston, New York, Philadelphia, and Newport cabinetmakers. Pendleton House, the "wing" of the Museum devoted to the exhibition of decorative arts, exhibits at least six pieces of furniture from the Goddard and Townsend circle of Newport cabinetmakers, including two of the renowned block-front, carved-shell desks-and-bookcases. Also on view in Pendleton House's period rooms are fine examples of English pottery, Chinese export porcelain, and a comprehensive survey of Rhode Island silver.

The Harold Brown Collection of French Empire furniture and objects with Napoleonic associations is another highlight of the department's holdings, as is the Lucy Truman Aldrich collection of rare 18th-century European porcelain figures. 360 examples of 18th- and early 19th-century French wallpaper from the M. and Mme. Charles Huard collection constitute the backbone of the Museum's wallpaper collection, which is among the finest in the world.

An extraordinary collection of silver (approximately 2,000 pieces) produced by Providence's Gorham Manufacturing Company from the mid 19th through the mid 20th century is the cornerstone of a fine collection of American silver that also includes work by colonial silversmiths such as John Coney, Paul Revere, and Samuel Casey.

The Museum's collection is particularly strong in the area of 19th-century decorative arts. Important highlights include furniture by the American companies of Vose and Coates, Herter Brothers, and Alexander Roux; the Englishman Edward William Godwin (E.W. Godwin); and the French makers Guillaume Beneman and Hugnet Frères. Other highlights of the 19th century are works of art in glass by Lalique, Louis Comfort Tiffany, and Hector Guimard; ceramics by Wedgwood, Sèvres, and Royal Doulton, and silver by Christopher Dresser, Charles Robert Ashbee and the Gorham Manufacturing Company.

20th-century design in the collection includes furniture by Alvar Aalto, Verner Panton, Josef Hofmann, and Charles and Ray Eames; metalwork by Erik Magnussen; ceramics by Auguste Delaherche, glass by Frederick Carder, and wallpaper designs by Nancy McClelland, Alexander Calder, and Roy Lichtenstein. The mid 20th-century's revived interest in "craft" is represented by the work of Tage Frid, Wharton Esherick, John Prip and Peter Voulkos. The RISD Museum is a leading collector of American contemporary craft and studio furniture and many of the artists represented in the collection have ties (either as alumni, faculty or both) to the School. Among the many contemporary craftspeople whose work is in the collection are: Dale Chihuly, Michael Glancy, Akio Takamori, Kurt Weiser, Judy Kensley McKie, Jere Osgood, Rosanne Somerson and Alphonse Mattia.

Painting and Sculpture

The Painting and Sculpture collection contains more than 2,500 works of European and American art from the medieval period to 1960. The Italian Renaissance and Baroque periods are represented by the work of Giovanni Battista Tiepolo, Lippo Memmi, Jacopo Sansovino, Alessandro Magnasco, and others. The collection also includes major work by such northern European masters as Tilman Riemenschneider, Hendrick Goltzius, Joachim Wtewael, Salomon van Ruysdael, and Georg Vischer.

17th- and 18th-century masterpieces include paintings by Francisco Collantes, Sebastien Bourdon, Gabriel-Jacques de Saint-Aubin, Nicolas Poussin, Angelica Kauffmann, and Joshua Reynolds. Early 19th-century European art is represented by Thomas Lawrence, Hubert Robert, Louise-Joséphine Sarazin de Belmont, Joseph Chinard, Théodore Géricault and others. The department has excellent examples of French Impressionism and Post-Impressionism schools by such artists as Edouard Manet, Claude Monet, Edgar Degas, Paul Cézanne, and Pierre-Auguste Renoir. There is important work by 19th-century French sculptors Auguste Rodin, Charles-Henri-Joseph Cordier, Jules Dalou, and Jean-Baptiste Carpeaux. Among the 20th-century European painters in the collection are Pablo Picasso, Georges Braque, Henri Matisse, and Raymond Duchamp-Villon, Fernand Léger, and Oskar Kokoschka.

The 18th- and 19th-century American collection is particularly strong, with important examples by such artists as John Singleton Copley, Gilbert Stuart, Thomas Cole, Winslow Homer, William Merritt Chase, Martin Johnson Heade, Mary Cassatt, John Singer Sargent, and Edward Mitchell Bannister, an African-American landscapist who spent his career as a painter in Rhode Island.

Significant works by George Wesley Bellows, Robert Henri, Charles Sheeler, Maxfield Parrish, Georgia O'Keeffe, John Twachtman, Hans Hoffman, Paul Manship, and Nancy Elizabeth Prophet, among others, represent American artistic achievements of the early 20th-century.

Prints, Drawings and Photographs

The department of Prints, Drawings + Photographs oversees approximately 18,000 European and American works on paper from the 15th century to the present. Included in the collection are important examples of Old Master drawings and prints, among them works by Giovanni Benedetto Castiglione, Giovanni Battista Tiepolo, Albrecht Dürer, Rembrandt and Goya.

The department has one of the largest collections (over 800) of British watercolors in the country. Included among them are fine examples by J.M.W. Turner, George Chinnery, John Sell Cotman, William Blake and Thomas Rowlandson. The collection of French prints and drawings includes work by Nicolas Poussin, Hubert Robert, Jean-Auguste-Dominique Ingres, Edouard Manet, Claude Monet, Honoré Daumier, Vincent Van Gogh, Paul Cézanne, Edgar Degas, Pablo Picasso and others. Notable in the collection of American watercolors and drawings is work by Benjamin West, Mary Cassatt, Thomas Eakins, Eastman Johnson, Winslow Homer, Maurice Prendergast and Maxfield Parrish.

Among the important 20th-century artists represented in the collection are Franz Kline, James Rosenquist, Helen Frankenthaler, Robert Motherwell, Jennifer Bartlett, Eric Fischl, Wayne Thiebaud, Kara Walker and Francesco Clemente.

The history of the art of the book is represented, in one of its earliest forms, by the Hypnerotomachia Poliphili (1499), a masterpiece of Renaissance illumination. In later centuries, work by masters of printing and illustration provides a link between the earliest books and twentieth-century "artists' books" that push limits and challenge traditional interpretations of the form. A summary of the history of photography is provided by 5,000 photographs, among them significant works by Gustave Le Gray, Julia Margaret Cameron, Nadar, Frederick Sommer, Carrie May Weems, and former RISD professors Aaron Siskind and Harry Callahan. The department also oversees the Aaron Siskind Center for the Study of Photography, which is open to photography students and Museum visitors alike.

Chief Ninigret
(1681)

Paul Bril, Self-Portrait
(1595-1600).

External links

- RISD Museum website [1]

- Media related to Rhode Island School of Design Museum at Wikimedia Commons

Geographical coordinates: 41°49′36.42″N 71°24′25.94″W

Old State House (Providence, Rhode Island)

Sixth District Court House (Old State House)	
U.S. National Register of Historic Places	
 Old State House in 2008	
Location:	150 Benefit St., Providence, Rhode Island
Built/Founded:	1762
Architectural style(s):	Georgian architecture
Governing body:	State
Added to NRHP:	April 28, 1970
NRHP Reference#:	70000092

The Old State House on College Hill in Providence, Rhode Island, also known as **Providence Sixth District Court House, Providence Colony House, Providence County House**, or **Rhode Island State House** is located on 150 Benefit Street. It is a brick Georgian-style building largely completed in 1762, and became the meeting place for the colony and state legislature for 149 years.

From colonial times into the mid-19th century, the Rhode Island General Assembly rotated meetings between the state's five county court houses, and five former Rhode Island state houses survive today. In 1760 The General Assembly built the Old State House to replace an earlier wooden courthouse built 1730 on Meeting Street. It was largely finished by 1762 with some details being completed by 1771. Many of the Georgian architecture details were borrowed from the larger and more ornate Newport Colony House. Before 19th century alterations to the Providence State House, the two buildings greatly resembled one another. After 1853 the state legislature ceased meeting at Kent, Washington and Bristol county courthouses, but continued to alternate its sessions between here and the Newport State House in Newport into the early 20th century.

At the Old State House on May 4, 1776, the General Assembly declared its independence renouncing its allegiance to the British crown, and the date is now celebrated as Rhode Island Independence Day. Fierce anti-slavery debates occurred in the building in the late 18th century. George Washington visited the building in 1781 and 1790. The building was extensively renovated and dramatically altered several times in the 19th century. By 1901 the new Rhode Island State House was occupied on Smith Hill and the legislature vacated the Old State House.

The Old State House was used as a Court House until 1975 and was listed in the National Register of Historic Places in 1970 and as part of the College Hill Historic Landmark District in 1971.

The building is now home to the Rhode Island Historical Preservation Commission.

See also

- National Register of Historic Places listings in Providence, Rhode Island

External links and references

- Main Website at Preservation RI [1]

Conley, Patrick T.; Jones, Robert B.; Woodward, William Ray (1988). *The State houses of Rhode Island: an architectural and historical legacy*. Providence, R. I.: Rhode Island Historical Society and Rhode Island Historical Preservation Commission. ISBN 0-932840-04-3.

Westminster Arcade

The Arcade	
U.S. National Register of Historic Places	
U.S. National Historic Landmark	

Location:	130 Westminster Street and 65 Weybosset Street, Providence, Rhode Island
Coordinates:	41°49′25″N 71°24′39″W
Built/Founded:	1828
Architect:	Russell Warren; James C. Bucklin
Architectural style(s):	Greek Revival
Governing body:	Private
Added to NRHP:	May 06, 1971
Designated NHL:	May 11, 1976
NRHP Reference#:	71000029

The **Westminster Arcade** or **Providence Arcade** (**The Arcade**, locally) was a historic shopping center in Providence, Rhode Island. It was the first enclosed shopping mall in the United States, built in 1828. It was closed in 2008 " in preparation for a major renovation of the mall's interior, according to the Providence Preservation Society", and remains closed.

History

Built by Russell Warren and James Bucklin in the Greek rectilinear temple style, the Arcade is replete with Ionic columns at either end. After falling into disrepair, it was rehabilitated by architects Irving B. Haynes & Associates and Gilbane Properies, and reopened in 1980.

Its three-stories were host to a diverse array of tenants including a number of primarily weekday lunch restaurants on the ground floor and a jewelry shop, a sci-fi/fantasy book shop, and local non-profits on upper floors.

It was declared a National Historic Landmark in 1976.

Gallery

Arcade interior, 2006

See also

- List of Registered Historic Places in Providence, Rhode Island
- Providence, Rhode Island

References

- Woodward, Wm McKenzie. *Guide to Providence Architecture*. Paperback. 1st ed. October 2003: United States. p84.
- Fodor's – Providence – Arcade [1]
- The City Rocks! Explore the Hidden World of Building Stone – The Arcade's Pillars: A Lost Sierra [2]

External links

- The Arcade, 130 Westminster Street, Providence, Providence County, RI: 2 photos, 5 data pages and supplemental material [3], at Historic American Building Survey

Providence Athenaeum

The **Providence Athenaeum**, founded in 1753 in Providence, Rhode Island, is the fourth oldest subscription library in the United States. Only the Library Company of Philadelphia, founded in 1731 by Benjamin Franklin, Newport's Redwood Library and Athenaeum, founded in 1747, and the Charleston Library Society, founded in 1748, are older. The Providence Athenaeum predates the New York Society Library, founded in 1754, and the Boston Athenaeum, founded in 1807.

The Providence Athenaeum, circa 1958. (U.S. Government Photo)

History

In 1753 a group of private citizens started the library to gain access to a collection of books that they could not afford individually. Members paid a small subscription fee to the library to purchase books which all members could share. Stephen Hopkins, signatory of the Declaration of Independence, was a leading member of the early organization. Many of the early books had to be purchased from England. In 1758, a fire destroyed the first collection of books, which were then housed at the Providence court house. Shortly after Brown University moved to Providence in 1770, the library offered students the use of its books. In 1836 the library merged with the Providence Atheneum (founded in 1831), and the merged organization became known as the Providence Athenaeum. In 1838 a new Greek Revival building was completed on Benefit Street by the Philadelphia architect, William Strickland.

References and external links

- Edward Field, *State of Rhode Island and Providence Plantations at the End of the Century: A History* (Mason Pub. Co, 1902) p.640, (accessed on google book search) [1]
- Providence Athenaeum official website [2]

List of Membership Libraries in the United States

Athenaeum of Philadelphia I Athenaeum Music and Arts Library I Boston Athenæum I Charleston Library Society I General Society Library I
Lanier Library Association I Mercantile Library Center for Fiction I Mercantile Library of Cincinnati I New York Society Library I Portsmouth Athenæum I Providence Athenaeum I Redwood Library and Athenaeum I Salem Athenaeum I San Francisco Mechanics' Institute Library I St. Johnsbury Athenaeum I St. Louis Mercantile Library I

List of Athenaeums in the United States

Philadelphia I Boston I La Jolla I Minneapolis I Portsmouth, NH I
Providence, RI I
Newport, RI I Salem, MA I Saint Johnsbury, VT I Columbia, TN I
Pittsfield, MA

Big Blue Bug

The **Big Blue Bug**, also known as **Nibbles Woodaway**, is the giant termite mascot of New England Pest Control, located along I-95 in Providence, Rhode Island. The Bug is 928 times the size of an actual termite, standing at 9 feet (2.7 m) tall and 58 feet (17 m) long, and weighing 4,000 pounds (1800 kg). It was constructed over a four day period from wire mesh and fiberglass in late 1980 at a cost of $20,000.

The Bug was originally painted purple (the color of an actual swarming termite when observed under a microscope), but the paint soon faded to a pale blue and the landmark became so well known in that condition that it was never repainted purple. The Bug has made numerous media appearances, including the film *Dumb and Dumber*, the television programs *The Today Show*, *The Oprah Winfrey Show*, *The Daily Show*, and *Family Guy*, the comic strips *Zippy the Pinhead* and *Bosquet*, and the books *Providence* by Geoffrey Wolff, *Roadside America* by Mike Wilkins, Ken Smith and Doug Kirby, and *Weird New England* by Joseph Citro.

The Bug was originally known only as the "Big Blue Bug," a name coined by Providence traffic reporter Mike Sheridan, until it received the name Nibbles Woodaway in a contest in 1990. Geraldine Perry of Tiverton, Rhode Island submitted the winning name.

The Big Blue Bug was built by Avenia Sign Company of North Providence,RI. Anthony Pescarino, Tom Grenga and Ronald Levesque assembled the sign over the course of a couple of months. Anthony Pescarino said, "we had to put the wings together and brought them to Valley Street to have them coated in fiberglass.". It was then assembled on site and then raised to the roof. The Big Blue Bug has also been featured on scratch-off lottery tickets, and was officially pardoned by Mayor Buddy Cianci for drinking Del's Lemonade (competitors of Del's claimed that the cup of lemonade was an impermissible billboard).

The Bug left its home on June 20, 2002 for a 5-stop tour. It was refurbished and painted a brighter blue before being returned to the roof of New England Pest Control.

Big Blue Bug Statistics

Species	Subterranean Termite (*Reticulitermes flavipes*)
Height	9 feet
Length	58 feet
Diameter	6 feet
Body Length	32 feet
Four Wings	40 feet (folded over in pairs)
Antennae	7 feet
Legs	11 feet
Weight	4000 lb
Stands	30 feet above ground

References

The bug was not fiberglassed on valley street. The bug was fiberglassed by Robert Garafano Sr who's company at the time was located on Delaine Street in Olneyville, Providence.

External links

- *New England Pest Control* home page [1]
- *RoadsideAmerica.com* Report on the Blue Bug [2]
- *Quahog.org* description of Nibbles [3]

Geographical coordinates: 41°48′25.5″N 71°24′20.0″W

WaterFire

The view of the City of Providence during WaterFire from Waterplace Park

WaterFire is the award winning sculpture by Barnaby Evans presented on the rivers of downtown Providence, RI.

First created by Evans in 1994 to celebrate the tenth anniversary of First Night Providence, WaterFire has grown to become an annual public art phenomenon.

WaterFire is simultaneously a free public art installation, a performance work, an urban festival, a civic ritual and a spiritual communal ceremony. Well known nationally and internationally as a community arts event, WaterFire's symbolism and interpretation is both inclusive and expansive - reflecting the recognition that individuals must act together to strengthen and preserve their community.

On WaterFire evenings, downtown Providence is transformed by one hundred bonfires that burn just above the surface of the three rivers that pass through the middle of downtown Providence in Waterplace Park (the Woonasquatucket, Moshassuck, and Providence rivers). The public is invited to come and walk the riverfront, and enjoy the beauty of the flickering firelight, the fragrant scent of aromatic wood smoke, the changing silhouettes of the volunteer firetenders, and the music from around the world – each of which engages the senses and emotions of all who stroll the paths of Waterplace Park.

Average attendance is 40,000 a night, ranging from 10,000 to 100,000. WaterFire is presented for free, with only ten percent of the funds needed to host WaterFire acquired through governmental means and the remainder coming from private and corporate donations.

WaterFire Providence

WaterFire Providence is the independent 501(C)(3) non-profit arts organization responsible for presenting WaterFire. WaterFire Providence consists of about 15 staff members and relies heavily upon volunteers for the production of WaterFire. On a given night, up to 160 volunteers make the entire event possible.

WaterFire History

Barnaby Evans created *First Fire* on New Year's Eve 1994 for the tenth anniversary of First Night Providence. *First Fire* consisted of 11 braziers on steel tripods stretching from WaterPlace Basin to Steeple Street. In June 1996, Barnaby created *Second Fire* for the Convergence Art Festival and the International Sculpture Conference.

Through the support of dedicated volunteers, WaterFire returned as a seasonal event. WaterFire gained regional attention and a coordinated effort to fund the project began. In 1997, WaterFire expanded to 42 braziers, and had an estimated attendance of 350,000 people over the entire season. Barnaby Evans received The Renaissance Award for his effort to revitalize downtown Providence, and WaterFire became the symbol of the city's renaissance.

For the 1998 installation, WaterFire expanded to include 81 fires, with expansions up the Moshassuck River and into the basin at WaterPlace Park. WaterFire now enjoyed national and international renown. Recently, attendance has increased from thousands to millions of visitors, with crowds reaching nearly two million per season.

WaterFire Programs

Ribbons of Light [1]
Luminaria Candle Lanterns [2]
Starry, Starry Night [3]
The Fire Flower Project [4]

Proliferation

- In June 1998 Barnaby Evans installed WaterFire in Houston, Texas on the Buffalo Bayou.
- In July 2005 Barnaby Evans designed a WaterFire installation in Columbus, Ohio, called WaterFire Columbus. http://www.waterfirecolumbus.com
- In 2007, Barnaby Evans created a new installaton in Kansas City, Missouri on Brush Creek near Country Club Plaza and the Nelson Atkins Museum of Art http://www.visitkc.com/waterfire.

External links

- WaterFire website [5]
- Washington Post travel article [6] by Carlo Rotella
- The Butterfly Effect blog entry [7] about WaterFire
- thisplaceiknow.com entry [8] for WaterFire

West End, Providence, Rhode Island

The **West End** is a neighborhood in the southwestern part of Providence, Rhode Island in the region often referred to as the South Side. Its boundaries are delineated by Westminster Street to the north, Huntington Avenue to the south, Elmwood Avenue to the east and the railroad tracks with Route 10 to the west. Cranston Street runs through the center of West End, past the Cranston Street Armory which has given the neighborhood the alternative name of the "Armory District."

History

The first settlement of the area took place shortly after King Phillip's War in the form of farming. In 1739, Obidiah Brown built the Hoyle Tavern at the intersections of Westminster and Cranston Streets, near present-day Classical High School. Early settlers built houses nearby to the tavern. In the 19th century, the area developed industrially and residentially with several factories built near the now-filled Long Pond. Residential construction followed after a horse drawn coach started serving the area in 1855 and a streetcar in 1865.

North of Cranston Street developed a white middle-class Yankee neighborhood of one and two family houses, while south of it, double and triple decker houses were built to accommodate increasing numbers of Irish, French Canadians, and blacks.

Following the urban decline of the 1930s, the West End has become a slowly decaying inner-city neighborhood as middle class residents left. The adjacent Huntington Industrial Park in Olneyville had kept industry nearby, but when Gorham Manufacturing Company left the area Olneyville lost importance as a freight rail hub. Further, Route 10 was constructed, physically separating the West End from the rest of the city.

In recent years, new residents have worked to improve and renovate the area's housing supply, particularly the more historic houses, including turning older houses into affordable rentals.

Demographics

As of the 1990 census, one in three residents of the West End was Hispanic, about 30 percent were African-American, and 14 percent were Asian, making the West End one of the city's most diverse neighborhoods. About one in three families was living below the poverty line and 44% of residents over 25 had completed high school.

According to the Providence Plan, a local nonprofit aimed at improving city life, half of all West End residents are Hispanic while 19% are African-American, 14% white, 13% Asian, and 1.6% Native-American. 68% of children under the age of six speak a language other than English as their primary language.

The median family income is $23,346, below the city-wide average of $32,058. 36.6% of families live below the poverty line while one in ten families receives some form of public assistance.

Nearly one in four children under the age of six have been exposed to high levels of lead.

Schools

Alfred Lima and Asa Messer Elementary Schools are both located in the West End area. Also, the West End Community Center, an afterschool program, is located on Bucklin Street.

References

Provplan.org *Neighborhood Profiles* [1]

Neighborhood Profiles at providenceri.com [2]

Smith Hill, Providence, Rhode Island

Smith Hill Historic District	
U.S. National Register of Historic Places	
U.S. Historic District	
Holden Street Providence, part of Smith Hill Historic District	
Location:	Providence, Rhode Island
Architect:	Unknown
Architectural style(s):	Italianate, Greek Revival
Governing body:	Private
Added to NRHP:	November 4, 1993
NRHP Reference#:	93001183

Smith Hill is a neighborhood in Providence, Rhode Island. Its traditional bounds are the Woonasquatucket River, the Chad Brown public housing complex, Interstate 95 and West River.

The Roger Williams Medical Center (RWMC) is located in the Smith Hill neighborhood and is adjacent to the VA hospital.

The Rhode Island State House is also located on the border with Downtown. The name 'Smith Hill' is therefore used as a metonym for the Rhode Island state government and the Rhode Island General Assembly.Wikipedia:Disputed statement[citation needed]

History

During the 19th and 20th centuries, Smith Hill became a densely populated area owing to its proximity to the Woonasquatucket and Moshassuck Rivers, which provided the power needed for the industrial mills.

Demographics

Christopher Dodge house, Holden Street, Providence

The neighborhood is home to whites of European descent and an increasing number of minorities. As of the 1990 census, Smith Hill was 20% Hispanic, 17.2% Asian and 12.2% black. The neighborhood's unemployment and poverty rates are above average for the city, though efforts have been made to revitalize the area.

Related links

Smith Hill Community Development Corporation [1], neighborhood non-profit dedicated to community building and affordable housing

References

- Providence Neighborhoods at Providenceri.com [1]

Attractions

Waterplace Park

Location	Providence, Rhode Island
Coordinates	41°49′25″N 71°24′27″W
Opened	1994

Waterplace Park is an urban park situated along the Woonasquatucket River in downtown Providence, Rhode Island. Finished in 1994, Waterplace Park is connected to 3/4 mile of cobblestone-paved pedestrian walkways along the waterfront known as Riverwalk. Venice-styled Pedestrian bridges cross the river. Most of Riverwalk is below street level and automotive traffic. Waterplace Park and Riverwalk together are host to Providence's popular summertime Waterfire events, a series of bonfires lit on the river accompanied by Classical and World music.

References

Woodward, Wm Mckenzie. *Guide to Providence Architecture*. 1st ed. 2003: United States. p 305.

Parks in Providence, Rhode Island

Burnside Park · India Point Park · Prospect Terrace Park · Roger Williams National Memorial · Roger Williams Park · Waterplace Park

Roger Williams Park

Roger Williams Park Historic District
U.S. National Register of Historic Places
U.S. Historic District
Dalrymple Boathouse

Location:	Providence, Rhode Island
Coordinates:	41°47′02″N 71°24′39″W
Built/Founded:	Feb. 12, 1872
Architect:	Cleveland, Horace William Shaler; Multiple
Architectural style(s):	Colonial Revival, Queen Anne, Other
Governing body:	Local
Added to NRHP:	October 15, 1966
NRHP Reference#:	66000002

Bandstand, Roger Williams Park

Roger Williams Park, in the southern part of the city of Providence, Rhode Island, is an elaborately landscaped 427-acre (173 ha) city park and National Historic District. The park is named after the founder of the city of Providence and one of the founders of the state of Rhode Island, Roger Williams. The land for the park was a gift to the people of Providence in 1871, in accordance with the will of Betsy* Williams, the great-great-great-granddaughter, and last surviving descendant of the founder to own the land. It had been the family farm and represented the last of the original land grant to Roger Williams in 1638 from Canonicus, chief of the Narragansett tribe. The family farmhouse (built in 1773), known as the **Betsy Williams Cottage**, and the Williams family burial ground (including Betsy's grave) are still maintained within the park.

- (While her headstone name spells as "Betsey Williams," through the centuries since she has been called "Betsy" as it appears on numerous articles, postcards, and books.)

The park also contains seven lakes which comprise approximately 98 acres (40 ha). It is located in the southernmost part of the city of Providence bordering the city of Cranston. The park was designed by Horace Cleveland in 1878, and was constructed in the 1880s. Many of the roads, bridges and sidewalks were built by the Works Progress Administration from 1935 to 1940. Currently it contains the Roger Williams Park Zoo, the Roger Williams Park Museum of Natural History and Planetarium, the Roger Williams Park Botanical Center, the Japanese Gardens, the Victorian Rose Gardens, the Providence Police Department's Mounted Command center, the Dalrymple Boathouse and boat rentals, historical tours, a Carousel Village for children that includes the "Hasbro Boundless Playground" which is accessible for handicapped children, the Temple to Music, the Roger Williams Park Casino, large greenspaces, and many miles of walking paths.

The National Trust for Historic Preservation has declared Roger Williams Park to be one of the finest urban parks in the U.S.

Images

Stereoview of the Betsey Williams
Cottage, built in 1782, contains an early
American flag supposedly stitched by
Betsey Williams

See also

- Roger Williams Park Zoo, third oldest in the U.S., and one of the top 20 zoos in the country
- Roger Williams National Memorial, a distinct park in downtown Providence
- Prospect Terrace Park, park located in Providence's College Hill neighborhood
- National Register of Historic Places listings in Providence, Rhode Island

References

Parks in Providence, Rhode Island
Burnside Park · India Point Park · Prospect Terrace Park · Roger Williams National Memorial · Roger Williams Park · Waterplace Park

Prospect Terrace Park

Location	College Hill, Providence, Rhode Island
Coordinates	41°49′47″N 71°24′25″W
Opened	1867

Prospect Terrace Park is a park located on Congdon Street in the College Hill neighborhood of Providence, Rhode Island. The park, founded in 1867, overlooks the city's downtown.

Author and Providence native H. P. Lovecraft frequently visited the park.

A statue of theologian Roger Williams was built in the late 1930s after Williams' descendant Stephen Randall made a deed of gift for the monument. The 35-foot stone statue commemorates Williams' founding of the state of Rhode Island and his promotion for religious freedom. The statue depicts Williams gazing over the city.

A plaque embedded in the sidewalk of the page contains a WPA logo

In 1939, Roger Williams remains were moved into a tomb that lies directly beneath the statue. His body had been overgrown by the roots of an apple tree next to his original grave. The roots grew over the form of his body, so that it looked identical to a human form. The remainder of his bones were reburied in a bronze casket and placed beneath his statue in Prospect Terrace. The so-called "William's Root" is preserved and is now on display at the John Brown House Museum on the East Side of Providence.

The statue itself and its supporting pillars have been substantially damaged by graffiti.

References

- City of Providence [1]
- Providence Prospect Terrace park Rhode Island [2]

Parks in Providence, Rhode Island
Burnside Park · India Point Park · Prospect Terrace Park · Roger Williams National Memorial · Roger Williams Park · Waterplace Park

Providence Bruins

Providence Bruins	
City	Providence, Rhode Island
League	American Hockey League
Conference	Eastern Conference
Division	Atlantic Division
Founded	1992
Home arena	Dunkin' Donuts Center
Colors	Black, yellow, white
Owner(s)	H. Larue Renfroe
General manager	Peter Chiarelli
Head coach	Rob Murray
Media	The Providence Journal, Providence Bruins Radio Network
Affiliates	Boston Bruins (NHL)
Franchise history	
1977–1992	Maine Mariners
1992–present	Providence Bruins
Championships	
Regular season titles	**2** (1998–99, 2007–08)
Division Championships	**4** (1992–93, 1998–99, 2002–03, 2007–08)
Conference Championships	**1** (1998–99)
Calder Cups	**1** (1998–99)

The **Providence Bruins** is an ice hockey team in the American Hockey League, and are the primary development team for the NHL's Boston Bruins. They play in Providence, Rhode Island at the Dunkin' Donuts Center.

History

The Providence Bruins began operation for the start of the 1992–93 AHL season after Providence mayor Buddy Cianci negotiated a deal with the owners of the Maine Mariners franchise, Frank DuRoss and Ed Anderson, to relocate their club.

The Bruins captured their first AHL Calder Cup in the 1999 playoffs, after a regular season in which they dominated the league with 56 regular season wins. Led by rookie head coach Peter Laviolette and paced by Les Cunningham Award winner Randy Robitaille, the Bruins went from only 19 victories the previous season, to dropping the Rochester Americans 4 games to 1 to skate away with the league championship.

In the 2001–2002 season, the Providence Bruins contracted with then-13-year-old musician Ben Schwartz to work as the official organist at all home games. As a result, Schwartz, who provided music for seven years until the conclusion of the 2007–08 season, holds the distinction of being the youngest organist to ever work for a professional North American sports franchise in history.

The Bruins will open the 2010-11 AHL Season with a home-and-home matchup against the Springfield Falcons. The Bruins will host on October 8, 2010 in Providence, and the Falcons will host on October 9, 2010 in Springfield. To honor the 75th anniversary of the American Hockey League, each team will wear throwback jerseys. The Bruins will wear the jerseys of the Providence Reds while the Falcons will wear the jerseys of the Springfield Indians.

This market was previously served by

- Providence Reds (1926–1977)

Team records

Single season

Goals: 41 Tim Sweeney (1992–93)

Assists: 74 Randy Robitaille (1998–99)

Points: 102 Randy Robitaille (1998–99)

Penalty minutes: 407 Aaron Downey (1997–98)

GAA: 1.84 Tim Thomas (2003–04)

SV%: .941 Tim Thomas (2003–04)

Career

Career goals: 101 ▬ Andy Hilbert

Career assists: 109 Andy Hilbert

Career points: 210 Andy Hilbert

Career penalty minutes: 1055 Aaron Downey

Career goaltending wins: 67 ▬ John Grahame

Career shutouts: 10 Tim Thomas

Career games: 278 🍁 Jay Henderson

Current roster

Updated October 13, 2010.

#	Nat	Player	Pos	S/G	Age	Acquired	Birthplace	Contract
4		Yury Alexandrov	D	L	22	2010	Cherepovets, Soviet Union	Boston
12		Jamie Arniel	C	R	21	2009	Kingston, Ontario	Boston
3		Matt Bartkowski	D	L	22	2010	Pittsburgh, Pennsylvania	Boston
2		Andrew Bodnarchuk	D	L	22	2008	Drumheller, Alberta	Boston
22		Joe Colborne	C	L	21	2010	Calgary, Alberta	Boston
30		Matt Dalton	G	L	24	2009	Clinton, Ontario	Boston
9		Zach Hamill	C	R	22	2008	Vancouver, British Columbia	Boston
35		Michael Hutchinson	G	R	21	2010	Barrie, Ontario	Boston
5		Steven Kampfer	D	R	22	2010	Ann Arbor, Michigan	Boston
25		Jordan Knackstedt	RW	R	22	2008	Saskatoon, Saskatchewan	Boston
18		Jeff LoVecchio	LW	L	25	2008	Chesterfield, Missouri	Boston
20		Lane MacDermid	LW	L	21	2009	Hartford, Connecticut	Boston
8		Nathan McIver	D	L	26	2010	Summerside, Prince Edward Island	Boston
6		Jeffrey Penner	D	R	24	2008	Steinbach, Manitoba	Boston
17		Jeremy Reich (C)	C	L	32	2010	Craik, Saskatchewan	Boston
7		Maxime Sauve	C	L	21	2010	Tours, France	Boston
31		Nolan Schaefer	G	R	31	2010	Yellow Grass, Saskatchewan	Boston
19		Wyatt Smith	C	L	34	2010	Thief River Falls, Minnesota	Boston
16		Jordan Smotherman	LW	L	25	2010	Corvallis, Oregon	Providence

37		Cody Wild	D	L	23	2010	North Providence, Rhode Island	Boston

Season-by-season results

Regular season

Season	Games	Won	Lost	Tied	OTL	SOL	Points	Goals for	Goals against	Standing
1992–93	80	46	32	2	—	—	94	384	348	**1st, North**
1993–94	80	28	39	13	—	—	69	283	319	5th, North
1994–95	80	39	30	11	—	—	89	300	268	3rd, North
1995–96	80	30	36	10	4	—	74	249	280	4th, North
1996–97	80	35	40	3	2	—	75	262	289	4th, New England
1997–98	80	19	49	7	5	—	50	211	301	5th, New England
1998–99	80	56	16	4	4	—	120	321	223	**1st, New England**
1999–00	80	33	38	6	3	—	75	231	269	5th, New England
2000–01	80	35	31	10	4	—	84	245	242	3rd, New England
2001–02	80	35	33	8	4	—	82	190	223	3rd, East
2002–03	80	44	20	11	5	—	104	268	227	**1st, North**
2003–04	80	36	29	11	4	—	87	170	170	4th, Atlantic
2004–05	80	40	30	—	7	3	90	211	202	4th, Atlantic
2005–06	80	43	31	—	1	5	92	254	217	4th, Atlantic
2006–07	80	44	30	—	2	4	94	251	218	3rd, Atlantic
2007–08	80	55	18	—	3	4	117	280	206	**1st, Atlantic**
2008–09	80	43	29	—	2	6	94	238	232	2nd, Atlantic
2009–10	80	36	38	—	5	1	78	207	226	7th, Atlantic

Playoffs

Season	Prelim	1st round	2nd round	3rd round	Finals
1992–93	—	L, 2–4, SPR	—	—	—
1993–94	Out of playoffs.				
1994–95	—	W, 4–3, PORT	L, 2–4, ALB	—	—
1995–96	—	L, 1–3, SPR	—	—	—
1996–97	—	W, 3–2, WOR	L, 1–4, SPR	—	—
1997–98	Out of playoffs.				
1998–99	—	W, 3–1, WOR	W, 4–0, HART	W, 4–2, FRED	**W, 4–1, ROCH**
1999–00	—	W, 3–0, QUE	W, 4–0, LOW	L, 3–4, HART	—
2000–01	—	W, 3–2, HART	W, 4–3, WOR	L, 1–4, SJNB	—
2001–02	L, 0–2, SJNL	—	—	—	—
2002–03	—	L, 1–3, MTB	—	—	—
2003–04	L, 0–2, PORT	—	—	—	—
2004–05	—	W, 4–2, MAN	W, 4–1, LOW	L, 2–4, PHIL	—
2005–06	—	L, 2–4, PORT	—	—	—
2006–07	—	W, 4–3, HART	L, 2–4, MAN	—	—
2007–08	—	W, 4–0, MAN	L, 2–4, PORT	—	—
2008–09	—	W, 4–1, PORT	W, 4–2, WOR	L, 1–4, HER	—
2009–10	Out of playoffs.				

Notable alumni

List of Providence Bruins alumni who played more than 100 games in Providence and 100 or more games in the National Hockey League:

- Nick Boynton
- Kevin Dallman
- Aaron Downey
- Peter Ferraro
- Jonathan Girard
- John Grahame
- Andy Hilbert
- Jamie Huscroft

- Milan Jurcina
- Cameron Mann
- Eric Nickulas
- Colton Orr
- Andrew Raycroft
- Jeremy Reich
- Wade Brookbank
- Randy Robitaille
- Jon Rohloff
- Andre Roy
- Cam Stewart
- Mark Stuart
- Tim Sweeney
- Tim Thomas
- Mattias Timander
- Landon Wilson
- Sergei Zholtok

External links

- Providence Bruins Official Website [1]
- Current Providence Bruins roster [2]
- The Internet Hockey Database - Providence Bruins [3]
- BBF Unofficial Site - Providence Bruins [4]

Dunkin' Donuts Center

The Dunk	
Former names	Providence Civic Center (1972–2001)
Location	101 Sabin Street, Providence, Rhode Island 02903
Coordinates	41°49′25″N 71°25′6″W
Opened	November 3, 1972
Owner	Rhode Island Convention Center Authority
Operator	SMG
Capacity	Ice hockey:11,075 Basketball: 12,500 Boxing / Center Stage: 14,000

Tenants
Providence Bruins (AHL) (1992–present) Providence Friars men's basketball (NCAA) (1972–present) URI Rams (NCAA) (?–2002) Providence Reds (AHL) (1972–1976) Rhode Island Reds (AHL) (1976–1977) New England Steamrollers (AFL) (1988) NCAA Men's Division I Basketball Championship (1976, 1978, 1979, 1980, 1981, 1985, 1989, 1996, 2010) NCAA Men's Division I Ice Hockey Championship (1978, 1980, 1982, 1986, 1995, 2000, 2003)

The **Dunkin' Donuts Center,** also known as **The Dunk,** is an indoor arena, located in downtown Providence, Rhode Island, United States.

Built in 1972 and originally known as the **Providence Civic Center**, the arena was built as a place for the emerging Providence College men's basketball program and the high demand for tickets to their games in Alumni Hall, as well as for the then-Providence Reds, who played in the nearly fifty-year old Rhode Island Auditorium.

The arena was known as the Providence Civic Center, until a naming rights deal was reached with Dunkin' Donuts in June 2001.

Current tenants include the Providence Bruins, of the AHL and the Providence Friars men's basketball team.

In December 2005, the Rhode Island Convention Center Authority purchased the building from the city of Providence and spent $80 million on an extensive renovation, to transform the facility into a state-of-the-art arena. Major elements of the construction included a significantly expanded lobby and concourse, an enclosed pedestrian bridge from the Convention Center, a new centerhung LED video display from Daktronics, new restaurant, 20 luxury suites, 4 new bathrooms, and all new seats with cupholders in the arena bowl. Behind the scenes improvements included a new HVAC system, ice chiller, and a first of its kind fire suppression system. These renovations were completed in 2008.

In 2010, the arena hosted first and second-round games of the NCAA Men's Division I Basketball Tournament for the first time since 1996.

Sports and events

A number of other professional sporting events (such as the Harlem Globetrotters), the 2008 NBA champions, the Boston Celtics in an exhibition game against the Cleveland Cavaliers, have been held at the Center.

The Providence Reds hockey team played there for five years starting in 1972.

It has been the site of many collegiate tournaments, including the inaugural 1980 Big East Conference men's basketball tournament; several ECAC basketball tournaments; NCAA men's basketball tournament first- and second-round games in 1976, 1979, 1980, 1981, 1989, 1996, and 2010; the 1978 and 1985 NCAA men's basketball regionals; the inaugural 1985 Hockey East Tournament (won by the home team) as well as the second tournament a year later in 1986 before the tourney made Boston a permanent home; and the 1978, 1980, 1982, 1986, 1995, and 2000 NCAA Frozen Four ice hockey championships. The University of Rhode Island also played home basketball games at Dunkin' Donuts Center, although this practice stopped with the opening of the Ryan Center in 2002. On rare occasions, the Providence women's basketball team has played "home" games in the arena, most notably for games against URI or UConn, where demand for tickets would be enough to warrant an arena larger than the 2,620-seat Alumni Hall.

The New England Steamrollers of the Arena Football League called the Center home for their single season of existence in 1988.

The Center has long been a regular stop on WWE tours. It was the site of WWF King of the Ring tournaments six times: (from 1986–1990) five times before the event became a pay per view, and once after in 1997, and hosted the 1994 Royal Rumble. On April 25, 1999, the Dunkin' Donuts Center was home to the first WWE Backlash Pay-Per-View event. In December, 2005 this venue hosted WWE

Armageddon. It also hosted Backlash (2009)

Artists that have performed at the arena include Elvis Presley, Grateful Dead, Phish, KISS, David Bowie, Queen, Bob Dylan, Led Zeppelin, Pink Floyd, Black Sabbath, Frank Zappa, Deep Purple, Yes, Elton John, Emerson, Lake & Palmer, Van Halen, The Police, Joan Jett & The Blackhearts, Prince, The Time, Vanity 6, Tina Turner, Ozzy Osbourne, Metallica, Queensrÿche, Metal Church, Alice in Chains, AC/DC, Whitney Houston, Jonathan Butler, Kenny G, After 7, Roger Waters, Robert Plant, Mötley Crüe, Def Leppard, Journey, Styx, REO Speedwagon, Bon Jovi, Rush, Primus, Bruce Springsteen & The E Street Band, Ronnie James Dio, Janet Jackson, U2, Pixies, Garbage, Cher, Celine Dion, Red Hot Chili Peppers, Aerosmith, Fuel, Lenny Kravitz, Jessica Simpson, Hilary Duff, Britney Spears, Christina Aguilera, Hannah Montana/Miley Cyrus, Jonas Brothers, Demi Lovato, David Archuleta, New Kids on the Block, Lady Gaga, Carrie Underwood, Josh Turner, Sons of Sylvia, Craig Morgan, Justin Bieber and American Idol Live!, among others.

The arena also hosted The Rolling Thunder Revue on November 4, 1975.

David Bowie's concert on May 5, 1978, was filmed & later released as a live album, titled *Stage*.

Gallery

View of the center while empty, after renovations

Arena in hockey configuration, after renovations

External links

- Official website [1]
- Naming rights deal press release [2]

This template requires you to use a title as the title parameter one of the succesion box headers as it's header parameter.

Transport

T. F. Green Airport

T. F. Green Airport Theodore Francis Green State Airport	
USGS aerial image	
IATA: PVD – ICAO: KPVD – FAA LID: PVD	
PVD	
Location of the T. F. Green International Airport	
Summary	
Airport type	Public
Owner	State of Rhode Island
Operator	Rhode Island Airport Corp.
Serves	Providence
Location	2000 Post Road Warwick, Rhode Island
Hub for	{{{hub}}}
Elevation AMSL	55 ft / 17 m
Coordinates	41°43′26″N 071°25′42″W
Website	www.pvdairport.com [1]

Runways			
Direction	Length		Surface
	ft	m	
5/23	7,166	2,184	Asphalt
16/34	6,081	1,853	Asphalt
Statistics (2008)			
Aircraft operations	108,392		
Based aircraft	72		
Source: Federal Aviation Administration			

T. F. Green Airport (IATA: **PVD**, ICAO: **KPVD**, FAA LID: **PVD**), also known as **Theodore Francis Green State Airport**, is a public airport located in Warwick, six miles (10 km) south of Providence, in Kent County, Rhode Island, USA. Dedicated in 1931, the airport was named for former Rhode Island governor and longtime senator Theodore F. Green. Completely rebuilt in 1996, the renovated main terminal was named for former Rhode Island governor Bruce Sundlun. It was the first state-owned airport in the United States.

Massport promotes T.F. Green as an alternative to Boston's Logan International Airport, as delays and wait time in the Rhode Island airport are minimal. PVD is the largest and most active airport among the six operated by the Rhode Island Airport Corporation (RIAC).

History

T.F. Green was dedicated on September 27, 1931 as Hillsgrove State Airport, drawing the largest crowd that had attended a public function in the country at the time. In 1933, the historic terminal building was built, located on Airport Road. It wasn't until 1938 that the airport assumed its current name.

During World War II, the Army Air Force took control of the airport from 1942 to 1945, using it for flight training for new air force cadets.

In the 1960s, the airport grew rapidly, as commercial aviation sought interest in the Providence market. The runways were expanded to accommodate jet airliners and a new terminal opened on Post Road. In the 1970s, most of the legacy carriers served T.F. Green. In the 1990s, T.F. Green's terminal was once again rebuilt, expanding to 18 gates and modernizing the infrastructure. In 1997, 4 gates were added, totaling the number of gates to 22. Airlines added service to T.F. Green, including Air Canada, Southwest, SATA International, and Spirit Airlines.

Following the September 11th attacks, T.F. Green, like most airports in the United States, faced a decrease in passengers, which resulted in fewer flights and loss of service, specifically from SATA,

American Airlines, and Spirit.

Facilities and aircraft

Theodore Francis Green State Airport covers an area of 1,111 acres (450 ha) at an elevation of 55 feet (17 m) above mean sea level. It has two asphalt paved runways: 5/23 is 7,166 by 150 feet (2,184 x 46 m) and 16/34 is 6,081 by 150 feet (1,853 x 46 m). Taxiway Victor served as Runway 5L/23R until 2003.

T.F. Green has a terminal with two concourses, North and South. The South Concourse has eight gates, and the North Concourse has 14 gates. Gate 7A is designed for international arrivals for use by Air Canada flights; it is directly connected to customs, which is on the lower level of the concourse. The terminal contains a number of stores and restaurants, and a central food court.

For the 12-month period ending April 1, 2008, the airport had 108,392 aircraft operations, an average of 296 per day: 45% scheduled commercial, 30% air taxi, 25% general aviation and <1% military. At that time there were 72 aircraft based at this airport: 76% single-engine, 6% multi-engine, 17% jet and 1% helicopter.

Providence is not considered a primary airport. Boston-Logan is New England's primary airport. However, some larger aircraft come into Providence's airport. US Airways uses either a A321-200 or a B757-200 for one of its five daily flights to Charlotte depending on the season. Delta Airlines also brings in a B767-300 during the football season for the New England Patriots.

Airlines and destinations

Airlines	Destinations
Air Canada operated by Air Georgian	Toronto-Pearson
Cape Air	**Seasonal:** Martha's Vineyard, Nantucket
Continental Express operated by Chautauqua Airlines	**Seasonal:** Cleveland
Continental Connection operated by Colgan Air	**Seasonal:** Newark
Continental Express operated by ExpressJet Airlines	Cleveland, Newark
Delta Air Lines	Atlanta, Detroit
Delta Connection operated by Atlantic Southeast Airlines	Detroit **Seasonal:** Atlanta

Delta Connection operated by Comair	Detroit **Seasonal:** Atlanta, Minneapolis/St. Paul
Delta Connection operated by Mesaba Airlines	Detroit **Seasonal:** Minneapolis/St. Paul
Delta Connection operated by Pinnacle Airlines	Atlanta [ends December 17], Detroit
Southwest Airlines	Baltimore, Chicago-Midway, Fort Lauderdale, Las Vegas, Nashville [ends November 7], Orlando, Philadelphia, Phoenix, Tampa **Seasonal:** Nashville
United Airlines	Chicago-O'Hare
United Express operated by Atlantic Southeast Airlines	Washington-Dulles
United Express operated by Mesa Airlines	Washington-Dulles
United Express operated by GoJet Airlines	Chicago-O'Hare, Washington-Dulles
United Express operated by Trans States Airlines	Chicago-O'Hare, Washington-Dulles
US Airways	Charlotte, Philadelphia, Washington-Reagan
US Airways Express operated by Air Wisconsin	Philadelphia, Washington-Reagan
US Airways Express operated by Chautauqua Airlines	Washington-Reagan
US Airways Express operated by Piedmont Airlines	New York-LaGuardia, **Seasonal:** Philadelphia
US Airways Express operated by Republic Airlines	Charlotte, Philadelphia, Washington-Reagan

Ground transportation

T.F. Green Airport has direct access to I-95 via the T. F. Green Airport Connector Road, a 1.1-mile (1.8 km) freeway. The airport is served by major car rental companies as well as by local taxi and limousine services.

The Rhode Island Public Transit Authority (RIPTA) offers public bus transportation to and from the cities of Providence (Kennedy Plaza in downtown Providence) and Newport. In particular:

* The #20 bus goes to Kennedy Plaza by way of Elmwood and Roger Williams Park and Zoo, and takes approximately 40 minutes.

- The #14 bus goes directly to and from Kennedy Plaza and takes approximately 15–25 minutes; it also connects to Newport, Narragansett, and East Greenwich.

New rail connection

Main article: T. F. Green Airport (MBTA station)

Construction has started on an intermodal station adjacent to the airport, which includes an elevated walkway to the terminal, a rental car garage, and commuter rail parking. The station is expected to be completed in September 2010, possibly with some MBTA service. Full MBTA Commuter Rail service - 8 trains every weekday - between Boston, Massachusetts and Wickford Junction is expected in 2011. These statements are forward looking and may not actually occur. A look at prior press releases indicates the station was to have been completed years ago. Amtrak has formally stated they will not stop at the station for the foreseeable future citing lack of being economically feasible.

Renovation/expansion plans

Terminal renovation project

Since the Bruce Sundlun terminal was opened in 1996, T.F. Green has become more congested due to increased traffic and post-9/11 security changes. As a result, terminal renovations have recently begun. According to the RIAC website, these improvements include:

- Expansion of the airline baggage rooms to accommodate the construction of a new In-Line Explosive Detection System (EDS) Baggage Handling System, allowing the removal of the EDS equipment currently residing in the terminal lobby;
- Expansion of the security screening checkpoint by widening the area to accommodate eight lanes and lengthening it to allow for increased passenger screening areas;
- Construction of exit ramps that will allow deplaning passengers to proceed directly to the lower level baggage claim area;
- Increased concessions on both pre- and post-security, including a new seating area in baggage claim on the lower level;
- Expansion of the second and third floor RIAC administration offices to accommodate RIAC staff and support space, TSA screening stations, and increased leasable space; and
- Addition of new ticket counter positions on both the north and south sides of the terminal lobby to accommodate future commercial service enhancements.

Runway expansion

The Rhode Island Airport Corporation writes (in 2001) that the master plan completed in 1997 failed to envision the "tremendous growth" that had been experience in the years hitherto. The report identifies lack of runway length as a hindrance to "range and diversity of service", in particular emphasizing ability to service non-hub locations, the west coast, and international locations. A challenge particular to T.F. Green in this regard is its being surrounded by dense residential and commercial development. Many local residents also oppose expansion for the impact it will have on quality of life in the area.

While some expansion proponents claim extending the main runway would bring in an estimated $138 million over the course of 13 years, doing so could consume 204 houses, at least ten businesses, and large areas of wetlands. More recent studies indicate substantially decreased enplanements due in-part to soaring fuel costs, and easier access to Logan International Airport since

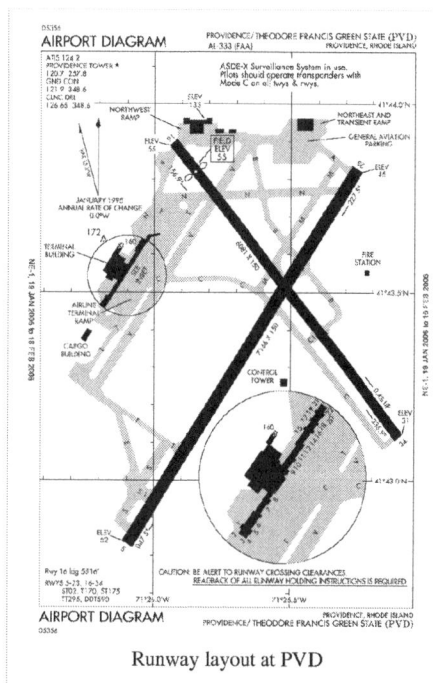

Runway layout at PVD

completion of improvements to the Southeast Expressway, Third Harbor Tunnel, bus services between TF Green and Logan, as well as the introduction of low cost carriers at Logan such as Jet Blue. The FAA plans to hold public meetings in upcoming May before making its recommendation concerning runway expansion to the Rhode Island Airport Corporation.

The Rhode Island Airport Corporation (RIAC) owns some residential property on the eastern side of the airport near the Aircraft Rescue and Firefighting building. Most homes on Cedar Swamp Road and Pembroke Avenue have since been demolished, likely to make way for future expansion.[citation needed]

Incidents

1999 runway incursion

On December 6, 1999 at approximately 20:35 Eastern Daylight Time, a runway incursion involving United Airlines flight 1448 (a Boeing 757) and FedEx Express flight 1662 (a Boeing 727) on Runway 5R/23L occurred. Shortly after landing on Runway 5R/23L, Flight 1448 was instructed to taxi to the gate. Due to the low-visibility conditions that night, the pilots became disoriented and turned down the wrong taxiway, which led them back towards the same runway. Flight 1448 then confirmed with the air traffic controller that they should cross the runway in front of them, and continued moving towards

Runway 5R/23L. The controller, not realizing their mistake, confirmed this crossing, then cleared another plane for takeoff.

Flight 1448 then reported that they were near taxiway Kilo, and as they re-entered Runway 5R/23L, reported that "somebody just took-off" overhead, referring to FedEx flight 1662 that had indeed just taken off, clearing the United aircraft. However, the controller appeared not to take their sighting of Kilo seriously, saying, "you shouldn't be anywhere near Kilo", and advised the 1448 crew to hold position. The Flight 1448 crew then informed air traffic control they were now on an active runway, which they mistakenly believed to be 23R (inactive at the time). A moment later the pilot corrected himself, stating that they were on 5R/23L. Flight 1448's crew were told again to stand by, so the plane remained idle at the intersection, while the controller cleared MetroJet flight 2998 for takeoff on the same runway. The 1448 pilot interjected to insist that the plane was on the active runway, which the controller denied, telling them it was not an active runway. The controller again told Flight 2998 to take off, but its crew, having listened to the exchange, realized there was confusion over the whereabouts of the United plane. They refused to take-off until Flight 1448 had made it safely to the gate.

The US Airways crew operating Flight 2998 were praised by a US Air spokesperson for their actions of avoiding a near-disaster. An investigation by the National Transportation Safety Board followed and while no fault was assigned to the controller, she was required to undergo retraining before returning to service. The pilots were debriefed by United, received additional training and were returned to service.

The NTSB generated a recreation of the events of that night.

2007 CRJ accident

On December 17, 2007, Air Wisconsin (US Airways Express) flight 3758 arriving from Philadelphia departed the left side of runway 5 after a hard landing by an unstabilized approach. Although the aircraft sustained substantial damage, none of the 31 passengers and crew aboard were injured.

Trivia

- The Rolling Stones were arrested here in 1972 after assaulting a photographer, and were brought to the Warwick police station. Their flight could not land in Boston, where they had a concert, due to fog. They were processed quickly to avoid a riot at the concert site.

See also

- Rhode Island World War II Army Airfields
- Rhode Island State Airport Terminal

References

⊚ *This article incorporates public domain material from websites or documents* [2] *of the Air Force Historical Research Agency.*

External links

- T. F. Green Airport [1], official site
- T. F. Green Airport Environmental Impact Statement (EIS) [1]
- Airfield photos of T. F. Green Airport (PVD) [2] from Civil Air Patrol website
- Aviation: From Sand Dunes to Sonic Booms, a National Park Service *Discover Our Shared Heritage* Travel Itinerary [3]
- Providence Journal video of a day in the life of the T.F. Green Airport [4]
- Horizon Aviation [5] (flight school located at airport)
- FAA Airport Diagram [6] (PDF), effective 23 Sep 2010
- FAA Terminal Procedures for PVD [7], effective 23 Sep 2010
- Resources for this airport:
  - AirNav airport information for KPVD [8]
  - ASN accident history for PVD [9]
  - FlightAware airport information [10] and live flight tracker [11]
  - NOAA/NWS latest weather observations [12]
  - SkyVector aeronautical chart for KPVD [13]
  - FAA current PVD delay information [14]

Providence Station

Providence		
Amtrak inter-city rail station		
MBTA commuter rail station		

Station statistics	
Address	100 Gaspee Street Providence, RI
Coordinates	41°49′45″N 71°24′48″W
Lines	Amtrak: *Acela Express* *Northeast Regional*MBTA: Providence/Stoughton Line
Connections	Bus routes
Baggage check	Available for Northeast Regionals 66 and 67

Other information	
Opened	1986
Accessible	♿
Code	PVD
Owned by	Amtrak

Traffic	
Passengers (2009)	582,296 ▼ 4%

Services

Preceding station	Amtrak	Following station
	Ⓣ **MBTA**	

Providence Station is a railroad station in Providence, Rhode Island and is served by Amtrak and the Massachusetts Bay Transportation Authority (MBTA). The station has four tracks for passenger service, with a fifth track passing through for Providence and Worcester Railroad freight trains. It is the 17th busiest Amtrak station in the country, after BWI.

Providence Station has full length high-level platforms and is wheelchair accessible. A new layover facility for MBTA commuter trains, located north of the station in Pawtucket, opened in 2006, allowing the MBTA to increase service to the city. Service is planned to T. F. Green Airport once a new station under construction in Warwick is completed September/October 2010.

History

Providence's first railroad station was Union Station, a brick edifice built in 1847 by the Providence and Worcester, Providence and Stonington, and Boston and Providence Railroads. This building was lost to fire in 1896, and replaced by a newer Union Station, completed 1898, which consisted of five large brick structures, built by New Haven Railroad. In 1986, the current Providence Station (shown here) was built to replace the 1898 station, as part of a redevelopment project to free up land from a mass of train tracks that had hemmed in downtown Providence. It is much smaller than its predecessor, reflecting the diminished local role of railroad transit. Designed by Marilyn Taylor of Skidmore, Owings and Merrill, local architectural historian William McKenzie Woodward lauds the building for its aesthetics, calling its saucer dome "an obvious yet very gracious gesture toward the (Rhode Island) State House".

The now-renovated buildings of the 1892 station still form the northern side of Kennedy Plaza in the center of Downtown Providence.

Amtrak

Two of Amtrak's passenger rail routes serve the station: the Acela Express and the Northeast Regional. The Acela Express is the United States' only high-speed rail service. It connects Boston's South Station with New York Penn Station and Washington, DC. The Regional rail service is a more local train that stretches between Newport News, Virginia and Boston. Not all Regional trains go to Newport News; the vast majority end at Washington, DC. 608,417 Amtrak passengers patronize the station annually.

MBTA

The Massachusetts Bay Transportation Authority (MBTA), also has service at Providence station. The Providence/Stoughton commuter rail line's southern terminus is located at Providence. The Providence/Stoughton Line provides commuter service to towns between Providence and Boston, sharing track with Amtrak trains. A new station is under construction that will allow service to T.F. Green Airport in 2010. Service might be extended farther south to Wickford Junction.

Unlike what the name implies, there is no direct service from Providence to Stoughton, Massachusetts. Stoughton station lies on a branch of the Providence/Stoughton line that is only accessible from stations between South Station and Canton Junction.

Ground transportation

A taxi stand faces the city side of the station. Though the Kennedy Plaza hub for bus-based local and regional transportation is approximately ¼ mile away, the route is not marked. The 50, 55, 56, and 57 RIPTA buses connect the state side of the station with Kennedy Plaza. Until the extension to the MBTA commuter rail is completed, those wishing to transfer to T.F. Green Airport via public transportation must take a bus to Kennedy Plaza and transfer there.

References

- Woodward, W[m] McKenzie. *Guide to Providence Architecture*. 1st ed. 2003: United States. ISBN 0-9742847-0-x. p303-304.
- *One Union Station* on The Rhode Island Foundation [1]
- Three and One-Half Centuries at a Glance (May 2002). [1] ProvidenceRI.com - History and Fact.

External links

- Amtrak - Stations - Providence, RI [2]
  - Ridership figures, FY 2008 [3]
  - Ridership figures, FY 2009 [4]
- MBTA Providence Station [5]
- Providence Amtrak-MBTA Station (USA Rail Guide -- Train Web) [6]

MBTA Commuter Rail

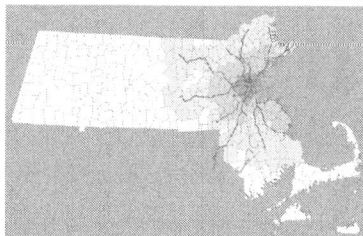

MBTA Commuter Rail

MBTA Commuter Rail provides commuter service from Boston as far north as Newburyport, as far south as Providence, and as far west as Worcester.

Reporting mark	MBTA
Locale	Eastern Massachusetts and Rhode Island
Dates of operation	1973–present
Track gauge	4 ft 8 $\frac{1}{2}$ in (1435 mm)
Headquarters	Boston, MA

The **MBTA Commuter Railroad** serves as the regional rail arm of the Massachusetts Bay Transportation Authority, in the United States. It is operated under contract by the **Massachusetts Bay Commuter Railroad Company** (MBCR) a joint partnership of Veolia Transportation, Bombardier Transportation and Alternate Concepts, Inc.. The current operating contract expires in July 2013.

The commuter rail system is the fifth-busiest commuter rail in the country, after only New York and Chicago area systems. The line's characteristic purple-trimmed coaches run as far south as Providence, Rhode Island, and as far north as Newburyport and as far west as Worcester, both in Massachusetts. The trains have two terminal stops in Boston—South Station and North Station—both transportation hubs offering connections to Amtrak, local bus and subway lines. As of Q1 of 2010, daily weekday ridership was 131,400.

Current lines

See also: List of MBTA Commuter Rail stations

The following lines have a terminus of South Station (listed from southeast to west):

- Greenbush Line
- Old Colony Line consisting of:
  - Kingston/Plymouth Line
  - Middleborough/Lakeville Line
- Fairmount Line
- Providence/Stoughton Line
- Franklin Line
- Needham Line
- Framingham/Worcester Line

The following lines have a terminus of North Station (listed from west to northeast):

- Fitchburg Line
- Lowell Line
- Haverhill Line
- Newburyport/Rockport Line

Operational history

The Commonwealth of Massachusetts's involvement with the operating facets of commuter rail began in 1967 when Boston & Maine petitioned the Interstate Commerce Commission to discontinue all passenger services. All service north of the state line was discontinued, but service in Massachusetts was preserved through a contract between the Commonwealth and the B&M, at this time still an independent railroad company.

The Boston & Maine Railroad (B&M), operator of the North Station commuter lines since the first half of the 20th Century, filed for bankruptcy protection in 1970. All B&M railroad assets inside Massachusetts Route 128 with the exception of yard tracks and freight-only branches were sold to the Commonwealth of Massachusetts in 1976. B&M was contracted to operate the service using its existing fleet of diesel railcars.

The New York, New Haven and Hartford Railroad (NYNH&H, or simply "New Haven"), the long time owner-operator of most South Station commuter trains, filed for bankruptcy for the last time in 1961. Just two years earlier in 1959, the New Haven had discontinued passenger service on the Old Colony division in southeastern Massachusetts. The New Haven was included in the Penn Central Transportation Company merger in 1968, which itself filed bankruptcy in 1970. During 1973-76, the Commonwealth of Massachusetts bought almost all track assets in Southeastern Massachusetts from the Penn Central's bankruptcy trustees.

The Worcester Line, historically part of the Boston & Albany Railroad (B&A), was merged into the New York Central System and its ownership subsequently passed to Penn Central in 1968. As part of the Massachusetts Turnpike Boston Extension's construction in the 1960s, the Worcester Line's right of way between Route 128 and Boston was sold to the Massachusetts Turnpike Authority, with the proviso that the control of the railroad remains with New York Central. Consolidated Rail Corporation (Conrail), Penn Central's successor, inherited the rail line which forms a vital freight artery between Boston's Beacon Yard and Conrail's Selkirk Yard. In September 2009, CSX Transportation and the commonwealth finalized a $100 million agreement to purchase CSX's Framingham to Worcester tracks, as well as some other track, to improve service on the Framingham/ Worcester Line. A liability issue that had held up the agreement was resolved.

The Northeast Rail Service Act of 1981 compelled Conrail to transfer operations of all passenger and commuter services to local transit authorities, resulting in Conrail ceasing all subsidized passenger rail services. The B&M won the contract for the South Side Lines also. After bankruptcy, the B&M continued to run and fulfill its contract under the protection of the federal bankruptcy court, in the hopes that a reorganization could make it profitable again. It emerged from the court's protection when the newly formed Guilford Transportation Industries (GTI) bought it, in 1983. GTI let the contract expire in 1986.

From 1986 to 2003, Amtrak managed all of Boston's commuter rail. MBTA observers saw Amtrak as having been a reliable manager and operator, but Amtrak sometimes experienced strained relations with the MBTA. Quibbles centered on equipment failures, crewing issues about the number of conductors per train, and responsibility for late trains. Because of these issues, and Amtrak's repeated statements that the MBTA contract was unreasonable, few were surprised at Amtrak's decision not to bid again for the MBTA Commuter Rail contract at its 2003 renewal.

When the MBTA asked for tenders on the commuter rail operation contract, Amtrak did not bid. Two tenders were submitted, from Guilford Rail System and from the Massachusetts Bay Commuter Railroad Company (MBCR), the latter of which won, taking over the MBTA Commuter Rail operation from Amtrak in July 2003. The MBCR contract originally expired in July 2008 but had an additional five-year option; it was extended three years to July 2011 and then another two to July 2013. After concerns about on-time performance, the 2011 extension increased the fine for late trains from $100 to $300.

MBCR partners Bombardier Transportation and Alternate Concepts have other ties to the MBTA. Bombardier is the manufacturer of much of the rolling stock operated by the railroad, while Alternate Concepts is majority owner of Paul Revere Transportation, which operates some bus lines under contract from the MBTA.

Service changes since MBTA takeover

Expansions

Many improvements have been made to the Boston Commuter Rail system during MBTA's period of stewardship which started circa 1973. However, it should be noted that the Commonwealth's support for rail operations began long before it owned the infrastructure, in the 1950s with contracted operations and subsidies to railroads providing commuter service.

- The Commonwealth of Massachusetts pioneered the concept of "Park and Ride" by providing funds to construct the Route 128 Station station on the New Haven Railroad's Providence Line, at a location where the radial line intersected with the Massachusetts Route 128, locally thought of as the Boston Beltway. Route 128 Station was established 1953 by New Haven President 'Buck' Dumaine. The initial station was simple in design, built as a parking lot located next to the tracks.

- During the 1980s reconstruction of the Southwest Corridor along MBTA's Providence/Attleboro Line, Amtrak trains between Boston and New York were diverted over the New Haven's Fairmount Branch. As part of this project, MBTA allowed Centralized Traffic Control to be installed on this branch, greatly increasing its signal capacity. Today, MBTA is in the process of constructing in-fill stations to better serve the urban neighborhood through which it passes.

- B&M's Newburyport Branch formerly operated across the bridge at Merrimack River and as far north as Portsmouth, New Hampshire on the former Eastern Railroad of Massachusetts alignment. At the time of the MBTA takeover, the daily service had been curtailed back to Ipswich, Massachusetts, and track north of that point downgraded if not abandoned entirely. In the 1990s, MBTA restored the service north to a point about 3 miles from Newburyport, Massachusetts.

- As part of the Northeast Corridor Improvement Program II (NECIP II) of the 1990s, MBTA's Providence Line was electrified using Federal funds provided to Amtrak for its Acela Express project. However, the MBTA does not operate electric equipment on the Providence Line, as such equipment would be unusable on other lines.

- At one time, MBTA's service reached only as far as Framingham, a suburb just beyond Route 128 about 12 miles from Boston. However, services on other lines reached exurbs more distant from Boston than Framingham. During the 1990s, an agreement was reached to extend MBTA's service out to Worcester, Massachusetts, making the line today's MBTA Worcester Line. During the early 2000s, trains only served Amtrak's Worcester Union Station beyond Framingham. Over time, several more in-fill stations were added in the MetroWest region. The service was successful, resulting in relative de-emphasis of Amtrak and commuter bus services operating in the same corridor.

- During the 1990s, MBTA invested heavily in the Commuter Rail system by restoring New Haven's Old Colony division abandoned in 1959. The two main Old Colony Lines were re-opened in 1997, and the Greenbush Line opened in 2007.

- Agreement with the State of Rhode Island allowed MBTA's Attleboro Line to extend to Providence, Rhode Island during the late 1990s. At first, only weekday service was provided. In the mid-2000s, a new agreement with RIDOT provided funding to allow the service to operate on weekends also.

Contractions

During the period of MBTA stewardship, services were also curtailed:

- All former B&M service that extended north of the Massachusetts border were curtailed by 1967. Since then, restoration and extension of the Lowell Line to Nashua, Manchester, and Concord, New Hampshire and the Haverhill Line to Portland, Maine have been repeatedly discussed. In 2001 Amtrak commenced operation of the *Downeaster* between Boston's North Station and Portland under the auspices of the Northern New England Passenger Rail Authority. The Nashua service discussion is continuing in the context of the widening of Interstate 93 in New Hampshire.

- Passenger service on the Arlington-Lexington-Bedford Line ended on January 10, 1977. The Alewife Extension of the MBTA Red Line replaced the service as far as Alewife in West Cambridge. No commuter rail service reaches the towns of Arlington, Lexington, and Bedford, Massachusetts. Today, the rail-banked line forms the Minuteman Bikeway and is a linear park in the vicinity of Davis Square, Somerville.

- The Lowell-Lawrence-Haverhill-Newburyport line had a Budd RDC-1 running on it well into the 1970s, but was discontinued when MBTA replaced the aging Budd equipment with more modern locomotive hauled trains. The route also saw one round-trip per day from Newburyport via Bradford, Andover, Reading to Boston in 1970.

- The Fitchburg Line under B&M operations terminated at Ayer, Massachusetts, but was subsequently extended as far as Gardner, Massachusetts. However, the service between Gardner and Fitchburg was ended when the parallel Massachusetts Route 2 was upgraded to expressway standards, dramatically reducing travel time between these cities.

- The southern half of the Woburn Loop still operated in 1970, joining the Lowell Line at Winchester. Half the Lowell Line services terminated at Woburn Heights (10.0 miles from Boston), while the others stopped at North Woburn (today's Anderson RTC) and continued to Lowell.

- As of 1970, B&M operated one daily round trip to South Sudbury (19.7 miles from Boston) over the former Central Massachusetts Branch, at this point curtailed to Berlin, Massachusetts. This service has since been abandoned.

Retired Equipment

As the Commonwealth assumed the control of the Commuter Rail during the 1970s, it inherited various non-standard equipment from predecessor railroads. These included:

- Numerous Budd Rail Diesel Cars, including a total of 86 from the B&M and several from the New Haven Railroad.

    The RDC fleet was de-powered in the 1970s and turned into locomotive-hauled coaches by Morrison Knudsen. These became known as "Boise Budds", after the location of the MK shop where the work was done. Remaining examples of these units now serve on the Grand Canyon Railway and Hobo Railroad.

EMD GP9 work train locomotive at South Station. This now-retired locomotive (No. 902) was transferred from the Southeastern Michigan Transportation Authority when the commuter rail operations were abandoned in Detroit.

- In 1978-80, MBTA acquired 19 rebuilt EMD F-units. EMD GP-9s were also operated in Boston suburban service. One of the EMD GP9's is still retained as a work engine (MBTA #904),one of the six GP-9s received from SEMTA in 1988.
- Ex-GO Transit stainless steel coaches were operated as an interim solution pending delivery of the CTC-1/BTC-1 order.

Amenities

- Free wifi is provided on all trains. The program started with a $262,000 pilot on the Worcester Line in January 2008.

Fare policy

The MBTA Commuter Rail uses a fare zone policy whereby origin and destination stations are not individually priced, but assigned a zone based on distance from Boston. There are a total of nine zones (1A, then 1 through 8) with an increasing fare to or from Boston the higher the zone number. Zone 1A fares are the least expensive and cost the same as rapid transit ($1.70), while the highest priced Zone 8 fares are $7.75 per ride. Travel between suburban zones without going to Boston is charged an "interzone" fare based on the number of zones traveled. Seniors, those with a disability, and middle and high school students with proper identification receive a 50% discounted rate; children under eleven travel free with a paying adult. Fares are collected by train conductors or the captain on-board and while fare evasion is explicitly illegal, it is not criminal.

Tickets may be purchased at automatic vending machines located in principal stations and at suburban stations from nearby businesses and vendors. Stations without ticketing machines or vendors can purchase tickets on-board. Travelers can purchase tickets as a one-way, round trip, twelve ride (no discount), or monthly pass (substantial discount over daily round-trip purchase).

Equipment

All MBTA Commuter Rail service is provided by push-pull trains powered by diesel locomotives. The current fleet of active passenger coaches numbers 410 ranging from 1978 to 2005, with an additional 75 on order from Hyundai Rotem to be delivered in 2010. There are a total of 83 active locomotives ranging from 1957 to 1993 with 80 being used for passenger service. Up to nine 2007 Motive Power locomotives are to be leased or purchased from Utah Transit Authority's excess fleet while the MBTA has placed an order with Motive Power for the purchase of 20 new units scheduled for delivery in 2012 and 2013.

Typical Commuter Rail train at Anderson Regional Transportation Center.

Passenger coaches are designated as either "blind trailer cars" (BTCs), which have no cab controls, or "control trailer cars" (CTCs), which have cab controls. All MBTA Kawasaki coaches are bi-level while the new Hyundai Rotem coaches will be bi-level as well.

Coaches

Year	Builder	Classification	Fleet ID	Seats	Restroom	Fleet Size	Notes
1978–79	Pullman	BTC–1C	200–258	114	No	57	Coaches 203 and 215 have been retired.
1987	Bombardier	BTC–1A	350–389	127	No	40	—
1987–88	MBB	BTC–3	500–532	186	Yes	33	—
1987–88	MBB	CTC–3	1500–1533	96	Yes	34	—
1989–90	Bombardier	BTC–1B	600–653	122	No	54	Rebuilt 1995–96
1989–90	Bombardier	CTC–1B	1600–1652	122	No	52	Coach 1648 has been retired. Cab controllers have been deactivated in coaches 1600–1626 making them BTCs.
1990–91	Kawasaki	BTC–4	700–749	185	No	50	—
1990–91	Kawasaki	CTC–4	1700–1724	175	No	25	—
1997	Kawasaki	BTC–4A	750–766	182	No	17	—

2001	Kawasaki	BTC–4B	767–781	182	No	15	—
2005	Kawasaki	BTC–4C	900–932	178	Yes	33	—
2010	Hyundai Rotem	BTC–5			Yes	0	75 on order for delivery in 2010.
				Total active coach fleet:		410	

Locomotives

Year	Builder	Model	Fleet ID	Horsepower	HEP[A]	Fleet Size	Notes
1957–60	EMD	GP9	902, 904	1750	No	2	Not used for passenger service
1971	EMD	GP40–1	3247	3000	No	1	Not used for passenger service
1973–75	GMD	GP40MC	1115–1139	3000	Yes	25	Rebuilt 1997
1978	EMD	F40PH	1000–1012	3000	Yes	13	Rebuilt 1989–90
1980	EMD	F40PH	1013–1017	3000	Yes	5	Rebuilt 1989–90
1987–88	EMD	F40PH–2C	1050–1075	3000	Yes	25	Rebuilt 2001–03. Locomotive 1073 damaged in a collision in 1990 and subsequently scrapped.
1991	MK	F40PHM–2C	1025–1033	3000	Yes	9	Rebuilt 2003–04
1993	MK	F40PHM–2C	1034–1036	3000	Yes	3	Rebuilt 2003–04
2007	MP	MP36PH–3C			Yes	0	Up to 9 to be leased or purchased from Utah Transit Authority's FrontRunner.
2012–13	MP	HSP46			Yes	0	20 on order for delivery in 2012 and 2013.
				Total active locomotive fleet:		83	

- A ^ Head End Power (HEP) provides electricity for the lighting, heating, and air conditioning of passenger coaches.

Ridership

Ridership levels on the Commuter Rail have grown since the MBTA's involvement began in the late 1960s, with overall average weekday ridership growing from 29,500 in 1969 to 76,000 in 1990 and 143,700 in 2008. This was accomplished by a series of rationalizations, such as closing lightly used lines, concentrating service on heavily utilized lines, and re-opening formerly abandoned branches with high traffic potential, such as the Old Colony Lines. A general growth of transit usage in the Northeastern United States also contributed. Growing ridership in this way required substantial capital investment, which was provided by a mixture of Federal mass transit funds and Commonwealth transportation bond issues.[citation needed]

Train operations

Like most commuter railroads in the Northeastern United States, MBTA is a NORAC Railroad and uses the Rulebook promulgated by that organization. Much of MBTA Commuter Rail is Rule 251 territory as the tracks are signalled for movement in one direction of travel only. During the 1990s, parts of the system were re-signalled to allow a more advanced mode of operations known as NORAC Rule 261, which allows trains to operate in either direction on both tracks where double track is available. During the morning rush hour, both tracks can be simutaneously used for inbound traffic, allowing one train to make local stops while an express train overtakes the local train.

On each train, the cab car is attached at the end closest to the downtown Boston terminal station for the particular line (either North or South Station), and the locomotive is attached at the end farthest from the terminal station. On each train serving the North Station lines, the "ADA" coach used to carry mobility-limited persons is attached right behind the locomotive, allowing level boarding at all suburban stations featuring mini-high platforms. On the other hand, on each train serving the South Station lines, the cab car also serves as the "ADA" coach. (The "ADA" coaches support compliance with the Americans with Disabilities Act of 1990.)

Trainlined doors that open automatically via central control are available on some equipment, but at low level platforms the conductor in each car must manually open a trap to allow passengers to descend via stairs onto the platform.

Proposed expansions

Several extensions of and improvements to the MBTA Commuter Rail network are in debate or under way.

South Station Lines

An extension of the Stoughton Line known as the South Coast Rail Link is set to break ground to bring service to Taunton, Fall River, and New Bedford, Massachusetts. Critics argue that building the extension does not make economic sense.

A Providence Line extension to T. F. Green Airport, in Warwick, Rhode Island, is under construction.

North Station lines

Littleton/Route 495 station in Littleton

There is a plan to extend and upgrade the Fitchburg Line. The extension would create a West Wachusett stop beyond Fitchburg Station. Upgraded high level platforms at both South Acton and Littleton are planned as well as enhanced drop-off and parking. No longer included is cab signaling but a second main track is planned between South Acton and Ayer Junction, which is shared with freight traffic, so that the Fitchburg to Boston trip would take only about an hour.

There is a proposal to build a South Salem Commuter Rail station in Salem, Massachusetts, to improve access to Salem State College, as well as to extend Commuter Rail to Peabody, Massachusetts and Danvers, Massachusetts.

The state Secretary of Transportation James Aloisi has also indicated support for commuter service from Worcester to North Station via Clinton and Ayer, presumably along the Worcester, Nashua and Rochester Railroad right of way, owned by Pan Am Railways as of 2009.

The state of New Hampshire has created the New Hampshire Rail Transit Authority and allocated money to build platforms at Nashua and Manchester.

An article in the *Eagle Tribune* claims that Massachusetts is negotiating to buy property which has the potential to extend the Haverhill Line to Plaistow, New Hampshire. Funding is available, and Plaistow is potentially interested, but wants to better understand the potential drawbacks of being the location of the layover station.

North-South Rail Link

No direct connection exists between the two downtown terminals; to travel from one station to the other, passengers must use the MBTA subway or the street. While passengers using the Providence/Stoughton, Framingham/Worcester, Franklin, and Needham lines can transfer to and from North Station at Back Bay via the Orange Line subway, all other passengers have to change subway trains at either Park Street or Downtown Crossing stations. A North-South Rail Link has been proposed to unite the two halves of the Commuter Rail system; but, because of the high cost, Massachusetts has, as of May 2006, withdrawn its sponsorship of the proposal.

Freight service

On the North Side lines, as part of the original sale agreement, B&M and its successor Pan Am Railways (formerly Guilford Transportation Industries) retains 'perpetual and exclusive' trackage rights for freight service. Pan Am provides freight service on those lines.

The shortline carrier New Hampshire Northcoast Railroad has an agreement with Pan Am to operate trains from Conway, New Hampshire to Boston's North Station to supply aggregates to the Boston Sand and Gravel plant on the Boston/Somerville border. An occasional move occurs with run-through power from Norfolk Southern Railway to supply coal to a power plant in Bow, New Hampshire, over the Fitchburg Line.

On the South Side lines, CSXT retains trackage rights over much of the former New Haven territory. Limited service is also provided by the Providence & Worcester, a regional railroad, on the Providence Line.

CSXT provides intermodal, autorack, and general merchandise over the Worcester Line, a part of CSXT's Boston Line. This part of the Commuter Rail network can host over 12 mainline freight trains per day, including descendents of Conrail's expedited intermodal Trail Van trains.

On its former Old Colony division, the New York, New Haven and Hartford Railroad (NYNH&H) essentially vacated its right of freight operations by abandoning the tracks in 1959. As MBTA rebuilt the tracks, it gained freight service rights, and those rights were franchised to Conrail (predecessor to CSX), which provided freight service on the former Old Colony division.

See also

- Big Dig (Boston, Massachusetts)
- List of United States commuter rail systems by ridership

External links

- MBTA Commuter Rail [1]
- Massachusetts Bay Commuter Railroad Company (MBCR) [2]
- MBTA Commuter Rail profile and photos [3]
- How MBTA rebuilt ridership [4] - Railway Age article from Nov 1991. Contains history of MBTA Commuter Rail system.
- MBTA daily rail operations visualized (Java applet, unofficial) [5]
- MBTA Fleet Roster [6]

Article Sources and Contributors

Rhode Island *Source*: http://en.wikipedia.org/?oldid=390397823 *Contributors*: 1 anonymous edits

List of counties in Rhode Island *Source*: http://en.wikipedia.org/?oldid=388707752 *Contributors*: GrahamHardy

History of Rhode Island *Source*: http://en.wikipedia.org/?oldid=390681884 *Contributors*: 1 anonymous edits

National Register of Historic Places listings in Rhode Island *Source*: http://en.wikipedia.org/?oldid=390018971 *Contributors*: Sanfranman59

First Baptist Church in America *Source*: http://en.wikipedia.org/?oldid=387594698 *Contributors*: Swampyank

The Breakers *Source*: http://en.wikipedia.org/?oldid=389703220 *Contributors*: UpstateNYer

Marble House *Source*: http://en.wikipedia.org/?oldid=380930306 *Contributors*: Doncram

Newport Tower (Rhode Island) *Source*: http://en.wikipedia.org/?oldid=386882974 *Contributors*: OpenFuture

Touro Synagogue *Source*: http://en.wikipedia.org/?oldid=380988852 *Contributors*: Skeezix1000

Newport Casino *Source*: http://en.wikipedia.org/?oldid=373569540 *Contributors*:

International Tennis Hall of Fame *Source*: http://en.wikipedia.org/?oldid=390566910 *Contributors*: TennisHallOfFame

Providence, Rhode Island *Source*: http://en.wikipedia.org/?oldid=390418644 *Contributors*: Tillman

Providence River *Source*: http://en.wikipedia.org/?oldid=360174695 *Contributors*: Colonies Chris

Providence County, Rhode Island *Source*: http://en.wikipedia.org/?oldid=385351427 *Contributors*: The Thing That Should Not Be

History of Providence *Source*: http://en.wikipedia.org/?oldid=390545862 *Contributors*: Orlady

Roger Williams National Memorial *Source*: http://en.wikipedia.org/?oldid=370033392 *Contributors*: Hmains

Veterans Memorial Auditorium (Providence) *Source*: http://en.wikipedia.org/?oldid=360756212 *Contributors*: Swampyank

Rhode Island School of Design Museum *Source*: http://en.wikipedia.org/?oldid=380338336 *Contributors*: Stev99

Old State House (Providence, Rhode Island) *Source*: http://en.wikipedia.org/?oldid=385478214 *Contributors*: Hmains

Westminster Arcade *Source*: http://en.wikipedia.org/?oldid=381601059 *Contributors*: Howlinwlf

Providence Athenaeum *Source*: http://en.wikipedia.org/?oldid=371685648 *Contributors*: Xb2u7Zjzc32

Big Blue Bug *Source*: http://en.wikipedia.org/?oldid=390677103 *Contributors*: 1 anonymous edits

WaterFire *Source*: http://en.wikipedia.org/?oldid=382261294 *Contributors*:

West End, Providence, Rhode Island *Source*: http://en.wikipedia.org/?oldid=333200979 *Contributors*: Hmains

Smith Hill, Providence, Rhode Island *Source*: http://en.wikipedia.org/?oldid=381191896 *Contributors*: Polaron

Waterplace Park *Source*: http://en.wikipedia.org/?oldid=373621992 *Contributors*: Marchela

Roger Williams Park *Source*: http://en.wikipedia.org/?oldid=365249388 *Contributors*: Chepiwanoxet

Prospect Terrace Park *Source*: http://en.wikipedia.org/?oldid=314019154 *Contributors*: DMacks

Providence Bruins *Source*: http://en.wikipedia.org/?oldid=390582919 *Contributors*: Officer pete

Dunkin' Donuts Center *Source*: http://en.wikipedia.org/?oldid=389777423 *Contributors*: Shyguy1991

T. F. Green Airport *Source*: http://en.wikipedia.org/?oldid=390056755 *Contributors*: Tofutwitch11

Providence Station *Source*: http://en.wikipedia.org/?oldid=371474130 *Contributors*: 1 anonymous edits

MBTA Commuter Rail *Source*: http://en.wikipedia.org/?oldid=388726110 *Contributors*: Grk1011

Image Sources, Licenses and Contributors

Image:Map of Rhode Island highlighting Kent County.svg *Source*:
http://bibliocm.bibliolabs.com/mwAnon/index.php?title=File:Map_of_Rhode_Island_highlighting_Kent_County.svg *License*: Public Domain *Contributors*:
User:Dbenbenn

Image:Map of Rhode Island highlighting Newport County.svg *Source*:
http://bibliocm.bibliolabs.com/mwAnon/index.php?title=File:Map_of_Rhode_Island_highlighting_Newport_County.svg *License*: Public Domain *Contributors*:
User:Dbenbenn

Image:Map of Rhode Island highlighting Providence County.svg *Source*:
http://bibliocm.bibliolabs.com/mwAnon/index.php?title=File:Map_of_Rhode_Island_highlighting_Providence_County.svg *License*: Public Domain *Contributors*:
User:Dbenbenn

Image:Map of Rhode Island highlighting Washington County.svg *Source*:
http://bibliocm.bibliolabs.com/mwAnon/index.php?title=File:Map_of_Rhode_Island_highlighting_Washington_County.svg *License*: Public Domain *Contributors*:
User:Dbenbenn

Image:Rhode-island-counties.gif *Source*: http://bibliocm.bibliolabs.com/mwAnon/index.php?title=File:Rhode-island-counties.gif *License*: Public Domain *Contributors*:
Original uploader was Jengod at en.wikipedia

Image:King Philip's Seat.jpg *Source*: http://bibliocm.bibliolabs.com/mwAnon/index.php?title=File:King_Philip's_Seat.jpg *License*: Public Domain *Contributors*:
Wikipedia:User:SwampyankSwampyank

Image:Roger Williams and Narragansetts.jpg *Source*: http://bibliocm.bibliolabs.com/mwAnon/index.php?title=File:Roger_Williams_and_Narragansetts.jpg *License*:
Public Domain *Contributors*: Lupo, Magicpiano, Origamiemensch, SonPraises, Ushistorynut

Image:John Greenwood - Sea Captains Carousing in Surinam.jpg *Source*:
http://bibliocm.bibliolabs.com/mwAnon/index.php?title=File:John_Greenwood_-_Sea_Captains_Carousing_in_Surinam.jpg *License*: unknown *Contributors*: Mattes,
Postdlf

Image:Samuel-Slater.jpg *Source*: http://bibliocm.bibliolabs.com/mwAnon/index.php?title=File:Samuel-Slater.jpg *License*: Public Domain *Contributors*: Akinom, Kam
Solusar, Man vyi, Shibo77, Verica Atrebatum, 1 anonymous edits

Image:Theodore Francis GREEN.jpg *Source*: http://bibliocm.bibliolabs.com/mwAnon/index.php?title=File:Theodore_Francis_GREEN.jpg *License*: Public Domain
Contributors: Original uploader was John English 9999 at en.wikipedia

Image:Rhode Island counties map.png *Source*: http://bibliocm.bibliolabs.com/mwAnon/index.php?title=File:Rhode_Island_counties_map.png *License*: Public Domain
Contributors: w:FedStatsFedStats

File:Beavertail Light, Jamestown, Rhode Island.jpg *Source*:
http://bibliocm.bibliolabs.com/mwAnon/index.php?title=File:Beavertail_Light,_Jamestown,_Rhode_Island.jpg *License*: Creative Commons Attribution 2.0 *Contributors*:
Lara

File:Joseph Reynolds House, Bristol, RI.jpg *Source*: http://bibliocm.bibliolabs.com/mwAnon/index.php?title=File:Joseph_Reynolds_House,_Bristol,_RI.jpg *License*:
GNU Free Documentation License *Contributors*: User:Daniel Case

File:Arkwright_Bridge_RI.jpg *Source*: http://bibliocm.bibliolabs.com/mwAnon/index.php?title=File:Arkwright_Bridge_RI.jpg *License*: Public Domain *Contributors*:
User:Marcbela

File:Pawtucket City Hall.jpg *Source*: http://bibliocm.bibliolabs.com/mwAnon/index.php?title=File:Pawtucket_City_Hall.jpg *License*: Public Domain *Contributors*:
User:Marcbela

File:First Baptist Meetinghouse, Providence, RI.jpg *Source*:
http://bibliocm.bibliolabs.com/mwAnon/index.php?title=File:First_Baptist_Meetinghouse,_Providence,_RI.jpg *License*: GNU Free Documentation License *Contributors*:
User:Daniel Case

File:USA Rhode Island location map.svg *Source*: http://bibliocm.bibliolabs.com/mwAnon/index.php?title=File:USA_Rhode_Island_location_map.svg *License*: Creative
Commons Attribution 3.0 *Contributors*: User:NordNordWest

File:Red pog.svg *Source*: http://bibliocm.bibliolabs.com/mwAnon/index.php?title=File:Red_pog.svg *License*: Public Domain *Contributors*: User:Andux

File:Breakers Gate.JPG *Source*: http://bibliocm.bibliolabs.com/mwAnon/index.php?title=File:Breakers_Gate.JPG *License*: Creative Commons Attribution-Sharealike
3.0 *Contributors*: User:UpstateNYer

File:Breakers Gardens.jpg *Source*: http://bibliocm.bibliolabs.com/mwAnon/index.php?title=File:Breakers_Gardens.jpg *License*: Creative Commons
Attribution-Sharealike 3.0 *Contributors*: User:UpstateNYer

File:Breakers Great Hall.JPG *Source*: http://bibliocm.bibliolabs.com/mwAnon/index.php?title=File:Breakers_Great_Hall.JPG *License*: Creative Commons
Attribution-Sharealike 3.0 *Contributors*: User:UpstateNYer

File:Breakers Library.JPG *Source*: http://bibliocm.bibliolabs.com/mwAnon/index.php?title=File:Breakers_Library.JPG *License*: Creative Commons
Attribution-Sharealike 3.0 *Contributors*: User:UpstateNYer

File:Breakers Kitchen.JPG *Source*: http://bibliocm.bibliolabs.com/mwAnon/index.php?title=File:Breakers_Kitchen.JPG *License*: Creative Commons
Attribution-Sharealike 3.0 *Contributors*: User:UpstateNYer

File:Cornelius Bedroom Breakers.JPG *Source*: http://bibliocm.bibliolabs.com/mwAnon/index.php?title=File:Cornelius_Bedroom_Breakers.JPG *License*: Creative
Commons Attribution-Sharealike 3.0 *Contributors*: User:UpstateNYer

File:Marble House, Newport, Rhode Island edit1.jpg *Source*:
http://bibliocm.bibliolabs.com/mwAnon/index.php?title=File:Marble_House,_Newport,_Rhode_Island_edit1.jpg *License*: GNU Free Documentation License
Contributors: Photograph taken by Daderot

File:Chineseteahouse.Newport.JPG *Source*: http://bibliocm.bibliolabs.com/mwAnon/index.php?title=File:Chineseteahouse.Newport.JPG *License*: Creative Commons
Attribution-Sharealike 3.0 *Contributors*: User:Ekem

File:Marble House - rear view facing sea, 1968.JPG *Source*:
http://bibliocm.bibliolabs.com/mwAnon/index.php?title=File:Marble_House_-_rear_view_facing_sea,_1968.JPG *License*: Public Domain *Contributors*: User:JGKlein

Image:DSCN3887 newporttower e.jpg *Source*: http://bibliocm.bibliolabs.com/mwAnon/index.php?title=File:DSCN3887_newporttower_e.jpg *License*: GNU Free
Documentation License *Contributors*: Original uploader was Decumanus at en.wikipedia

Image:Chesterton-1836.png *Source*: http://bibliocm.bibliolabs.com/mwAnon/index.php?title=File:Chesterton-1836.png *License*: Public Domain *Contributors*: Anon.

CPSIA information can be obtained at www.ICGtesting.com
Printed in the USA
LVOW01s0503031213

363572LV00016B/736/P